No Rules

What if Everything You Knew About Presentation Was Wrong?

By

Bob Caren

"Wise men speak because they have something to say; Fools because they have to say something"

Plato

Cover design & Photography by Mark Randall

Cover model – Julie-Ann Dean

Interior Model – Sue Randall

ISBN 978-1-326-24984-7

Published by Bob Caren

Printed by Lulu.com

Copyright © Bob Caren May 2015

All rights reserved. No reproduction, copy or transmission of this publication may be made without written permission.

No paragraph of this publication may be reproduced, copied or transmitted without written permission or in accordance with the Copyright Act 1956 (amended).

The material that is contained within this book is set out in good faith for general guidance. No liability can accepted for any loss or expense incurred as a result of relying on particular circumstances based on statements in this book.

The legal system, laws and regulations are complex and are liable to change over time. Readers should check the current position with the relevant authorities before making personal arrangements.

How to use this book

This book is designed to make it easy for you, the reader and presenter or speaker, to dip in and out of the topics listed in the contents. When I wrote this book I was very aware that most of my clients find it very difficult to find the time to read a whole book. You and I live in an age where there is never a point in the day when we sit down and say to ourselves "I seem to have finished all my work and don't have anything to do".

Instead it is much more likely that you will find that there is a certain problem or challenge you face at this moment in time and going to the specific point in the book may well be the way to answer the challenge you face.

If you do have the time then the book is presented in an order that at the time of writing seems to be the most logical way I would take a new student through the process of developing into a first-class communicator.

However you choose to read the book it is my intention that you will get a number of effective ideas that will help develop your own style to make you able to deliver your presentations and get the results that make you both very effective and someone who enjoys their presentations.

Contents

Foreword	2
Introduction	6
Chapter 1: Objectives	15
Chapter 2: Audiences	27
Chapter 3: Preparation for Presentation	37
Chapter 4: Some Theories on Memory & Memorable	48
Chapter 5: Opening & Closing a Presentation	66
Chapter 6: Making a Connection	86
Chapter 7: Selling and Buying	99
Chapter 8: Your Best Stage, Using Media & Priming Your Audience	110
Chapter 9: A Digression……	131
Chapter 10: ……..Into Storytelling	139
Chapter 11: Managing Yourself	149
Chapter 12: A Few Thoughts About Body Language	155
Chapter 13: Low Risk & No Risk Practice	167
Chapter 14: Getting Feedback & Excelling At Q&A	183
Chapter 15: A Few Thoughts On Writing	191
Chapter 16: Next Steps & Further Reading	194

Foreword by Rachel Bright

I'm sure I'm not alone in finding the prospect of standing on stage in front of an audience of almost a million people, somewhat daunting. Pretty much all of us have experienced - to some degree or another - the dry mouth, trembling limbs and churning stomach of being called upon to speak or perform to a group of people (whatever the size). This is magnified to potentially cold-sweat proportions when that group is one that you really, really care about making an impression on. This was exactly the position I found myself in before I met Bob.

Now, the nature of my day to day work is pretty much the polar opposite of public speaking. As a writer and illustrator, time alone to think, scribble and daydream is generally the rhythm of the thing. We, as a creative breed, are not generally famous for being comfortable as the centre of attention. But when I was asked to represent the UK as official World Book Day illustrator, it was an honour and an opportunity too good to miss.

With it came the exciting (and terrifying) responsibility of standing up in front of numerous groups to talk about the craft of storytelling. These events would ultimately culminate in a live televised celebration of books and reading at the Southbank in London on World Book Day.

I count myself very lucky to have been introduced to Bob in the nick of time – a coach who not only schooled me in the art of charismatic and memorable in-person communication, eliminating 90% of my nerves, but, more than that, transformed my experience of public speaking into something

I actively *enjoyed* and subsequently wanted to do again. And again.

This book is, in my opinion, the next best thing to having Bob by your side. All the techniques he reveals will help you distill the energy and emotions surrounding your presentations into light-up-a-room-rocket-fuel for performances that not only deliver what's needed but deliver it in style, making all your appearances memorable for all the right reasons.

He has a unique way of breaking down the key ingredients of effective communication, which makes a stellar performance a possibility open to us all. And this is at the heart of it...my best teachers have always empowered me to feel I was ultimately ready to tackle just about any situation myself. This is Bob's approach to teaching.

As Bob and I worked closely together on the run up to the big day, I think I must have fallen into just about every textbook trap a novice is vulnerable to along the way. My introductions lacked punch due to all the thanking-people-for-being there I was doing, my best and most engaging anecdotes hiding behind a little too much information padding, my grand finale felt slightly rushed...you name it...I did it, but with Bob's expert advice and guidance, all distilled in these pages, things began to change.

I prepared (which involved filming myself acting out the 5 minute presentation I had to give many times over and sending it over to Bob for feedback), I gradually got inside the minds of my primary audience (6-12 year olds with a short attention span, asked to sit still and listen for the best part of an hour) and my secondary audience (publishing professionals, teachers, booksellers, librarians, journalists and of course my fellow contemporaries) and I tweaked and tweaked. And then I practiced. And practiced some more (there really is no substitute for a bit of perseverance!).

On the morning of the big day, as I ignored my room service breakfast and paced my London hotel room, running through my talk a few final times, I felt the knots in my stomach tightening.

And then I remembered something Bob told me, 'if I'm right, you're beginning to imagine what might go wrong' he had said 48 hours before. He was right…my internal dialogue had recently begun gleefully holding up outsize mental neon arrows pointing at questions like, 'what if I forget everything?' and 'what if I trip on my way up to the stage?' and 'What if the kids get bored and there's a 6 year old heckler in the front row out for my blood?' (It happens)…'well, yes, a bit' I confessed to Bob. 'its human nature', he reassured, 'but I want you to try this…as soon as you get one of those thoughts, let it happen but then immediately indulge in a mental treat…follow it up with a best-case-scenario thought like, 'what if it goes better than expected? What if this is the start of a whole new chapter of public speaking? What if I have the time of my life?'

This turned out to be amongst the sagest advice I have ever been given. This simple thinking exercise starts to point you in the direction you want to go. It keeps your eyes on the prize. It allows you to craft a *positive* self-fulfilling prophecy.

The lights came up. The cameras rolled. Applause roared through the auditorium as Tony Robinson entered left and began proceedings, introducing some of the best-loved names in children's literature, 'put your hands together for Shirley Hughes (who created the Dogger books), Lauren Child (the mind behind Charlie & Lola)' and...'you're up' said the producer's voice in my earpiece...

The next 30 minutes are somewhat blurred in my mind. It went like a dream. It went better than expected. I enjoyed every minute. I couldn't wait to do it again.

Since then, with Bob's continued encouragement, I've been invited to speak in front of all kinds of audiences...corporate, educational...you name it, talking about how to make dreams a reality and turn your passion into a living, through the experience of my own journey (I now combine writing and illustrating children's books for the folks at Puffin, Harper Collins, Orchard & Walker with running my card & gift brand *'the brightside'*) and now...not only can add 'professional speaking' to my CV but also honestly say I absolutely love it.

I have Bob's techniques to thank for that and having read his book, which contains everything I learnt and more, I can tell you they really do work. So, happy reading, happy speaking and most of all happy enjoying-every-second-of-it.

Rachel Bright is an acclaimed Children's Author-Illustrator and head thinker-upper-of-ideas for her global card & gift brand *the bright side*. To find out more about Rachel and her work or invite her to inspire and motivate by speaking at one of your events, why not www.lookonthebrightside.co.uk

Introduction:

NO RULES
What If Everything You Knew About Presentation Was Wrong?

I remember the night of my first school play where I had a lead role. It was St Mary's primary school in Coventry, and our class was performing the 'Pied Piper of Hamlyn Town'.

I was one of two narrators. I remember being very excited as I stood behind my lectern with my words written in front of me. I'd been dressed in a snazzy green velvet jacket with a large dickie bow. I felt like I was 'the business'.

Sat in front of me was a sea of smiling faces mostly relatives of my classmates and me; parents, grandparents, uncles and aunts, older brothers and sisters, all waiting for those moments when their family member would appear, dance or speak onstage.

It was time to begin.........

"The rats, the rats, they fought the dogs, they killed the cats"

It is one of a number of childhood memories that flow easily to me. That was a particularly happy one. Our teacher had prepared us well and we'd practiced a lot. Everything I needed was in front of me and I felt comfortable and confident in how I looked and what I was about to do.

In those moments I was lost in all the things I was talking about and the positive reactions I got from the audience.

All I thought about was what I was doing now. I didn't think about anything that had been said and gone and I didn't think about what might be coming up over the next couple of pages. I thought about where I was now, I gave it my full attention and I gave everything I had.

I believe that this school play was the moment where I learned to love standing up and talking in public. My experiences since then have ranged from some truly awful performances to ones that have made me very proud.

Proud because they have moved people, proud because some audience members have found something for themselves that has improved their lives, even if only a tiny bit. And proud because I am doing what I love to do.

I have been inspired by many speakers from all walks of life, in one to one situations, meetings, and training and in larger audiences. A lot of those speakers have helped me get that little bit closer to my goals in life.

The book you are about to read is my take on all that I have learned and experienced in life with regards to speaking in public. I have distilled these experiences into something which I believe are the key things that will help you to develop your own skills.

These are the key skills and strategies that are at the heart of my approach to bringing the best out of speakers. I have tried these methods over the past 40 years, 15 of them as a presentation coach, consultant, facilitator and trainer. This has been done with people at all levels, in all types of industries such as pharmaceuticals, dental and medical, agriculture, agency and consultancy, retail, education, hair and beauty, engineering and entertainment.

I want you to be able to deliver effective communication more often. And I want your life to be made easier by spending the right amount of time preparing, so that you get the value and reward for the investment of your time.

Throughout my various jobs and careers, I have had numerous times where I have had to communicate with individuals and groups about information of varying importance to both me and them. And yet for long periods of my life I didn't consider the importance of the communication. I only considered the amount of time I had, or could be bothered to spend, in preparing for it.

Peter Thomson, the author of many excellent programmes and an inspiration for me, introduced me to the idea of away and toward motivation through his brilliant Achievers Edge audio programme.

The idea is that roughly 95% of us are more naturally away motivated. That means if we are in an uncomfortable situation then we will be motivated to take action to move away from that situation.

However, that motivation goes when our situation becomes tolerable and we feel comfortable again. That is despite the fact that in order to move away from that uncomfortable situation we may well have done things outside our own comfort zones and had experiences that you think would give us confidence to try more and push further on.

So for example, an away motivated person has a presentation coming up. They have two weeks' notice but they are quite likely to only get to work on it the day before they need to deliver it. If during that time they discover that they could have added a compelling video to their presentation that would have made a great difference to them but needed more time, it is highly likely that next time they face a similar challenge they will still be thinking the day before that they could have done a video.

The other 5% are the ones who are towards motivated.

These are the ones who have a major positive goal ahead of them and will continue to be motivated until that goal is complete. These people are likely to continue to set new goals and are more often moving forward, breaking new ground and importantly making mistakes doing it!

More importantly they learn from these mistakes and they continue to look to move forward.

So, what am I? (It's funny thinking about the array of answers that are popping into your head right now!). I need to create a lot of pain to motivate myself to take action. I'm very much one of the 95%. I'm somebody like you.

The likelihood is that you've picked this book up because you are not in a comfortable place about some aspect of presenting. It may be that you don't like presenting. It may be that it actually terrifies you. Or it may be that you do it but you don't get the results you would like. Maybe you don't think you are as good at it as you would like to be.

So what will you get from reading this, and from investing some of your time and some effort?

You will develop the **best performance of you**. You will know how to hit highs in your presentations so that you and your audience enjoy and understand the messages so that you are consistently an effective communicator.

And I want you to be able to do this whilst remaining authentic to who you are. You will achieve this through learning, understanding and practice. This creates a **path of positive progress** for you.

I have been presenting for over 40 years in some shape or form. The last 15 years have seen me learn, practice, make mistakes, learn more, make more mistakes and importantly have a lot of success.

I've met and worked with people at all levels of experience and capability with regards to presenting. I have made a difference for so many people. Some differences were small and many were large differences.

My most enjoyable times have been when I have worked with people, eager to learn and prepared to practice. It is with those people that I have shared some really great successes.

The progress for you depends on what you want and how much you are prepared to practice for yourself. I want to work with you to bring about progress and success, whether it's getting you through a testing time now or whether it's part of a longer term plan for you.

And I want to work with you as a guide that you can dip in and out of over a longer period of time.

In this book I will provide for you a valuable approach to assessing the value of communication to you. The book has techniques for making your presentation work for you and your target audience.

It will help you to deliver the best performance of you and teach you about using low-risk, no-risk practice that will boost your communication confidence and give you a lot of fun on the way.

During the course of this book you may well be surprised to note that more senior people who present to you aren't as good at it as you may have thought.

Throughout the chapters you will understand the mistakes that practiced presenters are making and how they impact on audiences. You will be more aware that the presentations you take for granted as 'good practice' really aren't!

Maybe the way other colleagues, directors and managers present is wrong? Maybe not all the time but more often than you would think. After today you should question what has been communicated to you when you attend presentations and meetings.

If someone asked you "What was that about?" as soon as you left a presentation or meeting, what would you say? And would it match what the communicator wanted you to say?

In this book I will give you my take on all my years of training, reading, listening, practicing and performing.

I do this so that you can short cut some mistakes and unnecessary experiences and get to a higher level quicker as a result of it.

Writing this book is not an easy task for a member of the 95% away motivated group. It's taken me longer than I'd have thought or wanted. I've had a lot of starts at it but I have picked up a lot of hints and tips from people along the way that have made this book possible. For those interested in writing a book for themselves I'll add those hints, tips and people in at the end.

I'm writing this book now because I encounter more and more people who are where I was in terms of communicating with little purpose. At this stage I can see that there is value in providing this information now.

I have processed all the information and experiences that have worked for me and organised them into the contents of this book. There are some of you who think the same way I do about presenting who will find most of the book useful.

There are some of you who will find a number of the ideas and approaches useful. The important thing is that by the time you have read this book and practiced the techniques, you have realised the value that it has added to you and your performances in presenting.

Every book I read, audio programme I listen to or training course I attend needs to deliver value for me. Value for the time and money I invest. Value for me is not in the amount of stuff I get. Value for me comes in getting ideas that I can practice and I know that they will make a positive difference for me.

When I first went into business for myself I made a commitment. That commitment was that 20% of my time and money would be invested in my continuing education and development.

It was a commitment I could easily make and stick to because I was my own boss. If you are your own boss I hope you have your own commitments. If you work for someone else it may feel that your time is often not within your own control. I hope that the ideas and experiences in this book help you have to spend less time to make progress.

When I was about to go into business for myself Simon Gulliford, a marketing consultant, gave me an enormously valuable piece of information.

He said "if you are going to be a success, keep giving away what you know! If you do that, it will force you to keep going out and finding something new!"

In my time as a coach, trainer, speaker and consultant these words have been hugely valuable. I have been lucky enough to have trained with some extraordinary people who have adopted this principal. I have followed those people and their work because they are always breaking new ground and always bring fresh perspectives and value.

In this book it is my intention to give away the main things I know about effective presentation and how to give the best performance of you.

As well as intelligent and successful people like Simon, I have also encountered those people who have a system and stick with it. They believe it is a secret unknown to the rest of the world. They hold onto it and teach it to people as a hard and fast rule.

The world, its rules and conventions are changing. Some die out, some move in cycles. Trying to hold onto unmoveable ideas is a formula that I believe leads to disappointment. The rules and conventions of our lives are not black and white.

One of the major challenges I face day to day is helping people move on from advice given by people who teach that the world of presentation is black and white and that there are rules.

I help to release clients from the hard and fast rules and systems that have been taught to them by well-meaning coaches and trainers with limited knowledge or interest.

One of the most important things I can tell you is that when it comes to effective communications there are no rules!

I will repeat that because I want to make sure that you understand this.

WHEN IT COMES TO EFFECTIVE COMMUNICATIONS, THERE ARE NO RULES!

Effective communications is about having good approaches that mean you consider your objectives, your audience, your environment and yourself and you use them to the benefit of you and your audience.

It's about having a variety of approaches to presenting that mean you can communicate with different audiences, in different situations and be able to deliver in all instances.

If you are very particular about your grammar rules, I'll warn you now; I talk more than I write and in this book I have chosen to write as I talk.

So that means quite a number of sentences end with prepositions. My role here is to communicate ideas and inspire you to give great presentations for you and the people who listen to you.

In the world of effective communication you are always striving to present for your audience. If you are particular about your grammar then I have broken some of those rules.

This just goes to show there are no rules!

If you can overcome the grammar issue, I'm sure you will find a lot that is helpful to you in this book.

Enjoy the book, find something you like, practice and give your best performance!

Chapter 1
Objectives

For many years I worked in the marketing department of Adams Childrenswear. A childrens clothing store that was very successful through the 80s and 90s.

The first job that really made going to work interesting, rather than just paying the bills and working with nice people, was in market research.

I loved trying to understand why people did what they did when they shopped. I loved trying to understand how they processed all this information. And how that made them love one thing and hate another.

I was fascinated by how, in groups, people's opinions could be so influenced, suppressed and even changed by the attitude and behaviours of people they had never met before.

And I loved the challenge of taking all this information and turning it into some useful advice or direction for the business. More of this later.

At the time I was the only one in the business working directly on consumer research. I had been well schooled by some excellent work colleagues; Karen Bycroft and Bill Allen and by some excellent people at a market research agency called Research International; Maureen Johnson and Helen West.

It was an area that I was passionate about and so the chance to stand up in front of groups of people and talk about my passion was something that I jumped at doing.

I should add that the thought of standing up in front of senior directors or large groups of people, excited me and terrified me in equal measure.

Very often we would work with a market research agency. They would pull together a PowerPoint report that they would present to the board. These presentation decks would often be prepared knowing that the presentation was likely to be very interactive.

Once the board had had their presentation, the next stage would be for me to cascade this information to the rest of the business.

The preparation process was very simple. The PowerPoint deck was the starting point. I would remove those slides that were for board-eyes only, and that was my presentation.

These presentation decks weren't designed to tell a story. Instead they were the key findings and the slides were mostly graphs that demonstrated these issues and opportunities. These charts were meant to create debate and discussion.

The way I used the deck was more as an uninterrupted tell session than an interactive meeting. It really should have had much more work done with it to make it into a narrative for different audiences.

And as I'd heard this presentation before I waited until the day I presented without any more practice. For a lot of the time I was just reading what was on screen.

It didn't matter whether you were accountants, sales managers, Distribution centres or human resources you were going to get the same presentation with the same deck.

In hindsight, what I had was a collection of facts and ideas that rarely connected into a narrative and was primarily designed for an audience for the purpose of interactive discussion.

I'd apologise now to those audiences for the number of times I presented to them about information and ideas that mostly had no relevance for them but instead gave them a different way to waste their time.

I hold back slightly on my apology because they and many others have paid me back with long, tedious and irrelevant presentations that have wasted my time.

There is an excellent sketch by the writer and comedian Armando Iannucci where he adds up all the irrelevant parts of his life and works out that 44% of his life has been a waste of time!

Think how much of your life has been wasted by pointless meetings and presentations where someone has wanted to share information that has been useless to you or so poorly presented that it has been as good as useless.

If you think about all the other people who have had the same experiences, the money they were paid and the positive opportunities wasted whilst listening to this stuff, you start to rack up a huge waste of time and money.

Then also take the larger conferences that businesses put on. Some pay six figure sums to put these events on. They then take hundreds of senior managers out of the business for a day or more. Then having done all this they then bombard them with things that a group of people wanted to say to them without much care as to what they, the audience, want or need to know.

Worse than this, those badly planned and prepared presentations cause misdirection because you end up doing what you thought the presenter wanted, not what they actually wanted.

You will probably not be surprised to know that if you don't do what was asked, the presenter is likely to put that down to the audience being stupid.

Surely stupidity is knowing a couple of hundred people have not understood your message and then thinking it must be their fault!

If you or your businesses are spending a huge amount of time and money on these events wouldn't you want to ask yourself if you wanted your event to be an expense? Or an investment?

Yet, over the 15 years I've been a coach the amount of time and money wasted on communication has probably increased to an eye-watering sum! At times I have felt like I am swimming against a strong tide of verbosity and time-wasting. I have lost count of the number of 'snorefests' that I have had to sit through.

Each new generation of workers enter these cultures of talking at people. They make the mistake of thinking this is how you communicate. It must be right because all these senior people present this way, surely they couldn't all be wrong?

And yet what they are doing is talking at an audience with information important to the speakers but often not important or relevant to their audience.

If you take a moment now and think about the range of communication you get, then ask yourself 'how much of that information actually changes or helps anything that I do?'

How much would you like to be different?

How much better would you want your presentations to be?

How much better could your presentations be for your audiences?

So what is the secret? The secret is that anytime you have to communicate to any number of people you need to ask yourself what are the objectives of this communication.

You're probably thinking it doesn't sound like much of a secret. Years ago I would have agreed with you. With a lot less experience I was looking for secrets to be magical. The sorts of things that made jaws drop and people say "wow".

But this secret has made the biggest difference time and time again. When someone I work with realises that answering the key question about objectives will suddenly make them understand what they have to do, it's at that point that I see the light bulb moment. After the lightbulb moment comes the confidence and surety that this can be a good and rewarding experience for them and their audience.

So what do you need to do?

You need to ask yourself what you want your audience to think, feel or do as a result of this communication.

Let me explain;

Maybe you are pigeonholed at work. A good presentation can make your audience think that there is more to you than your role allows you to demonstrate. So your objective is to get the relevant senior people to appreciate what you can offer and how what you do makes a significant difference in your business.

Maybe you are aware that your managers think that promoting you might be a risk. A good presentation can make them feel more confident that you can make it work. Here your objective may be to demonstrate through previous examples of your work and life experiences that you can operate at a higher level.

Maybe you need more resource to deliver on a great opportunity. A good presentation can make your business do the right thing and give you the resource you need. Here your objective could be to get your audience to understand the value of the project.

Let me give you an example. 6 years ago I was asked to talk at an Event Conference by an agency I was working with. They were exhibiting at the event and wanted more people to come and talk to them.

My job was to do a talk around the broad topic of social media. The talk was to a broad audience from many different industries. My objective was to make them **think** that we understood how to entertain and inform audiences. To make them **feel** they had used their time well by gaining useful information and that the agency would be easy to talk to without hard sell. And what I wanted them to do was to talk to the agency as a result of being inspired by their experience (**Do**).

With that objective I wanted to communicate to the audience that the agency was open, that it understood how to do events for an audience and it knew how to make connections.

I used this to create a 45 minute interactive session that had no hard selling. The agency's logo was used on the start and finish of the brief Powerpoint presentation. And business cards and brochures were placed around the room.

The audience were told a few interesting and relevant stories relating to the use of social media, taught a magic trick and actively involved all the way through. At the end lots of the audience stayed to talk and got in contact with the agency people at the event.

I had the opportunity to talk to them and ask them about what they had got from the session. They told me that they had got value from the content of the session, that they had enjoyed the time and that they had appreciated that the presentation was not all about the agency and had no hard sell.

Most importantly they then asked about how to get in touch with the agency. Objectives achieved!

Other people would have taken that talk and spent 5 minutes talking about social media (the reason that audience had come along to this talk) and 40 minutes about what a great agency they are.

Achieving good results can happen when you are clear about what the objectives are for this particular part of the process of communication. You can focus your presentation to present only what you need to achieve your objectives.

This means a more focused and relevant presentation for your audience that means you are not wasting their time or yours. And you will know at the end of it whether you have been successful and got the result you wanted or needed.

You will be amazed by the number of people who do not think about why they are communicating. They don't know when to stop because they are not clear as to why they are doing it.

One of the most obvious places this occurs in is selling.

Clearly the ultimate objective for sales people is making sales. However, selling is often done in stages. The techniques necessary to get a meeting or even 5 minutes of somebody's time is very different from the techniques necessary to ask for a large order.

Sales people fall down often because they try to overshoot their real objective, they push too far, too fast because their objectives and the setting they are in are unclear to them.

If you are meeting somebody you have never met before and they are unclear about whether or not you can provide them with something that will make their life easier, then the first step for a salesman could be to introduce enough of a hook to get this potential client to agree to a longer meeting.

The first meeting you have could be about them learning enough about you to be able to trust you and believe what you have to tell them. The objective for this could be to get a second longer meeting. The second meeting might be to discuss possible projects or opportunities.

If you met someone who you were attracted to how many of you would suggest getting married five minutes after meeting them? There are a number of stages to go through but going straight to the ultimate purpose can be a very bad choice to make. Maybe objective one is to have a coffee together. And then see what happens from there.

It seems so obvious to know why you would communicate but it is often overlooked. If you take the time to understand your objectives you can give the communication some value.

This will help you to give it the appropriate time and the right level of preparation.

If communication is of low value it helps you to think about how much time it is worth for you and your audience. And this will help you to trim the fat off the communication so you get to the heart of why you are communicating.

The wonderful thing about clear objectives is that you will be amazed by how often you can discover that a meeting or presentation is a waste of time for all involved. Then you can get that valuable time back for something really worthwhile.

It is a really powerful positive experience to make someone realise that the presentation that they think they want you to do is actually of little value to anyone. The only reason it's done is because it seems that it's always been done.

Apparently people supposedly more senior and intelligent than you have gone along with this for years and you could be the first one to wake everyone up to the fact that they were all wasting their time!

So the next time you are asked to do a presentation, take a little time to consider your objectives.

Think about what you want your audience to think, feel or do as a result of your presentation. It might be about an idea, a product, a project or it might be specifically how they relate to you.

Once you know your objective then give it a relative value. For instance, is it necessary to get peoples agreement so that you can carry on with the next stage of your work? Is this a situation where your audience will be interested in buying your product once they realise the impact it can have on them? Is this like an interview where your performance will go a long way toward you getting that promotion you so dearly wanted?

If the answer is yes to any of these questions then it only makes sense that you would give yourself the time you need to prepare for an impactful presentation. Preparation is covered in chapter 3.

And of course what if it has no value to you or the people you are talking to? Clearly now you might want to assertively challenge this.

"What do you think will change for me or the audience as a result of doing this?"

"Am I going to be wasting their time by taking them through this?"

"If you were doing this presentation, what would you want the audience to think, feel or do differently as a result of it?"

These are some questions you could politely ask to make the person giving you the job snap out of their trance and try and think how everyone's time could be better used. If they can answer any of these questions then at least it gives you a clear direction. However, you will be amazed at the number of times such a question gets a blank response because the person asking you to do the presentation has never given it that much thought.

Sometimes you just have to do it!

I worked in corporate businesses for a long period of time and I understand there are a lot of senior people who aren't doing what they love. They don't care for their job but they have grown use to the lifestyle. They have lost a little bit of self-confidence and don't believe they could do something they enjoyed and be paid enough for it.

People like this may well just tell you to do it because "it has to be done!", "it's always been done!", "they will complain if we don't do it!"

So you want to keep your job and keep your boss happy. My advice is to spend as little time preparing as is necessary to 'get through'.

Try and have some fun with it and try and make it as short as is possible for an audience who are probably not keen on having their time wasted.

There are some upside opportunities for you if you want to invest some time. This could be an opportunity to practice something new that you want to try out to improve your own performance. There is always something positive you can get from this situation.

In summary; every time you need to present think clearly about the objectives. If the presentation has the potential to make a big difference for you and your business then put in good preparation and practice time.

If the presentation has no value to you or your audience, try and reason with the person who is asking you to do it. Failing that, find the shortest and easiest way to deliver it and minimise the pain for you and your audience.

Alternatively use these sorts of presentations to practice something new.

Knowing the objectives of your communication is vital if you want your communication to be effective!

Actions: From now on when you are running a presentation or meeting write down the objectives. Why is it of value to you and why is it of value to your audience.

Make the time to ask speakers that you have listened to what were their objectives for their presentation. See if they matched your take on the presentation.

Chapter 2
Audiences

It's funny how when it comes to communicating the overriding compulsion to be liked by most, if not all, people comes to the fore. It's just something that is naturally built into us. You and I meet people in all sorts of situations and find that before we realise it we are going to some lengths to get a stranger, who we may never meet again, to like us.

Now in principle I think this is a good thing. The world might be a happier place if we all set out to be nice people. The unfortunate thing is in this world there are quite a few people who know this and like to use it to their advantage and not for a mutual benefit.

I'm assuming you are somebody who is interested in mutual benefit.

In this chapter I'm going to ask you to be a little bit more selfish in your thinking so that you can bring a little bit more benefit to you and others. As a good and reasonable person I'm sure you're aware that it is a path worth taking.

The first job I did that I loved was market research. However else my life develops the market researcher in me will not lie dormant. I'm interested in people. I'm interested in what they are motivated to do and why they do it. I'm interested in knowing if they know why they do things or is it something they do without thinking.

When I concentrate I'm a very good listener. And if you are a good listener you know that if you pay attention and listen; really listen, people will tell you way more than they would expect to!

Whilst being a market researcher, I spent years having total strangers tell me, in some detail, their television preferences, their shopping choices, why they buy some greetings cards and not others, their medical histories, the colour and type of underwear and the significance of wearing different pants.

They would tell me about how they were affected by shops, restaurants, adverts and people. And they would have told me much more if I had given them the time.

When I started my business I spent a lot of time attending all types of presentations and talked to the speakers and the audiences about what they had seen and heard. I was looking for what made communication work and what helped communication to fail.

I have asked them about lots of things but in this chapter I will concentrate on the subject of why they were there.

The main reasons they told me why they had attended a presentation were:

Because of who was giving the presentation
Because of what they are talking about
Because of what they needed to learn for their benefit

Many audience members can quite rightly point to any combination of the reasons above and say that is why they were there. Valid reasons all.

However there were 2 other common reasons why people go to presentations:

To be seen to be there

Because they were told to be there

These two reasons are important because more audience members than you would expect will cite these reasons for their attendance.

Let's take the first one: **To be seen to be there.**

Status is very important to a lot of people and particularly in business. Again other people's opinions of you and I tend to matter to us more than is sometimes healthy.

So if I have a peer group. That is people who sit at a similar level of achievement, let's say a group of managers, then it might well matter what meetings I get invited too. If it's a big meeting, upwards of 100 people, then if anyone from the peer group is invited you may well expect that entire group to be invited.

If some names are left off, then those that care about status will fight tooth and nail to be included in that meeting. That is regardless of content that may be of little importance to them.

Not to be there might be an admission of inferiority within the peer group. So let's say they convince the relevant person of their need for an invite then you, as the speaker, have an audience member who probably has little interest in the content of the meeting but one who has satisfied their ego. The person leading the meeting now has someone in the room with little or no interest in their subject!

The second group are the **ones who were told to go**. Their boss thought that there is something that they need to hear, maybe not directly relevant to them but possibly that person will be able to make a connection between what they hear at the presentation and what they do for a job.

This group of people may or may not find the presentation valuable and they may or may not listen.

It's fair to say that even the best presenter with a great presentation might struggle to make a difference to these two groups of people, a well-considered and delivered presentation will have a target audience in mind. Sadly, these two groups often provide audience members that are not a target for the presenter or their topic.

The post presentation feedback from these groups often ranges from "that was interesting" (but I'm not going to do anything with it) to "I don't think that was relevant to me" and beyond to "that was boring!"

I refer to this group as being your **Tertiary** audience.

You, the effective speaker, are less interested in their feedback. Instead, you will want to make sure that your **Primary** and **Secondary** audiences have got your message and will respond in a way that works for you.

So who are your **Primary & Secondary** audience?

Your primary audience are the main people you are directing your presentation at. They are usually the decision makers. They might be the ones who can spend money, who can approve recruitment and resources and who can make the connections that are necessary for you.

It is vital that they are informed, inspired or moved to action by your presentation because the success, or not, relies on them responding in a way that achieves your objectives.

The secondary part of the audience is those that have influence over your primary audience. Lots of people take advice or are swayed by the thoughts and influence of others.

A well-crafted presentation will consider what is necessary to make the influencers positive about your messages.

Any information you can get about who influences your primary audience is vital.

One of the most regular areas this occurs in is if you are trying to sell an idea to creative people but it is going to need some financial investment. The final decision may well rest with the creative team. But the finance people could influence whether or not it goes ahead by presenting the impact on cash and profit.

In this case, including information that satisfies the finance part of the audience, whilst still inspiring the creatives, will greatly improve your chances of success.

Understanding who your audience is matters. You need a presentation that will move your audience to respond in the way you want. To do this you have to have messages that feel like they are specifically aimed at that target audience.

Most experienced presenters who do not want help with or feedback about their presentations are usually the ones who do not consider their audience. These people think they don't need help because they have the confidence to stand up and talk to large groups of people.

They talk about what they know without considering who they are talking to and what is useful or relevant to that audience. And their attitude is "If the audience doesn't understand then it's their fault!"

Effective presentations talk to the primary and secondary audience because they are the ones who are the key to achieving your objectives. The more you dilute a presentation in order to avoid upsetting people or avoid annoying those who are from the tertiary part of your audience, the blander your presentation becomes.

And the blander your presentation, the less likely you are to move your primary audience to action. I have lost track of how many presenters have diluted their message or added boring additional information because they do not want to upset someone who is neither a decision maker nor an influencer.

So make sure you understand how your audience is made up. Get to know who is who in your organisations and with your clients and customers. Ask questions because the more you find out the better you can target your presentation and then you can really improve your results.

I can remember doing a presentation to a room of over 200 people where my primary audience was 1 person, my secondary audience was 1 person and the other 200 odd were my tertiary audience.

I hope I didn't bore the tertiary audience but I'm not overly concerned if I did because I know I hit home with my messages to my primary and secondary audience.

One of the most important reasons why you should know your audience as well as you can is because for the majority of your presentations they are the single most important element.

A successful presentation depends upon you getting your audience to think, feel or do your objectives.

For people like you and I our presentations have to be focussed on delivering to what an audience wants. We have to know what important need our communication can solve.

Way too many presentations are filled with what the speaker wants to say and not what the audience needs to hear. Do your research. Understand the key issues that your communication needs to address. If you aren't able to do this you are guessing as what might make a difference.

If I am addressing an audience whose biggest concern is confidence and I am talking to them about tips for Powerpoint slides, then chances are I might not be hitting the mark on effective communication.

Knowledge of your audience will also help you to shape content.

You need to know their level of understanding and familiarity with your topic so that you can talk at the right level of detail.

If I'm listening to a presentation about a computer programme I don't need to know about the coding, the engine that runs it or any of that level of detail. I need to know what it can do for me, and how easy is it to work with as a user.

If however, I work in the systems area and I am going to have to integrate that into existing systems then the detail is going to be of huge value to me.

In my time I have sat through way too many presentations that have gone into too deep a level. I warn you now; the vast majority of senior managers, directors, entrepreneurs and business owners will not tolerate their valuable time being wasted.

Do your research and remember that what your audience needs to hear is often way more important than what you think you would like to say!

One other thing I would like you to think about is how do you address your audience.

When it comes to preparing what you might say remember that your audience is made up of a lot of individuals rather than just one mass called 'the audience'.

It is really good to think of you addressing your audience as if you are addressing them one to one.

Imagine you are listening, engaged and connected to a speaker and their message. The speaker then addresses you as "all of you."

Now you are sitting there thinking 'I'm not an all of me, I am just me'.

As you consider what you might say, think of one person and you will find that the language, tone and body language you use is much more engaging and rapport building for your audience.

One other really important thing that I would like you to consider is the roles that you and your audience play during your presentation.

What I mean by this is that you have to ask yourself a couple of important questions.

Who am I to the audience?

Who is the audience to me?

Before you start to prepare your presentation you need to think about these questions. Let's consider them.

So when I stand up and talk am I one of them? Do they see me as a voice for them? Am I an expert on my subject? Do they see me as someone with credibility so that my focus is only on my key messages? Or do they see me as an unknown quantity where I have to prove myself to them before I can talk about my key messages? Am I an authority figure? Do they see me as someone that they need to listen to?

What about the relationship of the audience to me. Are they Pupils? Peers? Friends? Formal acquaintances?

When you answer these questions it allows you to prepare your presentation. This helps you to understand what your communication challenge is and what you need to overcome to communicate successfully.

It helps to set the right tone and it also helps you to keep a consistent feel throughout your presentation because you retain the role you have set at the outset.

Get to know as much as you can about your audience; ask questions to people in the know. If you can ask questions of the primary audience you are making your life and their life much better and much easier

Action:
Who are the primary people that have to get the message?

Who are the secondary people that will support your message?

And let everyone else, the tertiary, take what they want from your presentation.

Ask good questions and find out who you are talking to!

Who are you to them? Who are they to you?

A great presentation is designed for the audience not for the speaker.

Chapter 3
Preparing For Presentations

In the early 90s I took up amateur theatre as a hobby. Like countless others I love watching great actors whether it be stage, film or television. It's brilliant when an actor can get you drawn into a story and actually make you care about them and their fate.

So, I thought this would be a great opportunity to learn, practice and perform in front of paying audiences. I was a little scared because I was concerned that I might not be very good at it.

When I did my first show, William Shakespeare's Midsummer Night Dream, I was just delighted to get to the opening night knowing my lines, my cues, where I was meant to be and what I was meant to do.

Because it was my first show I dragged any family member, friend or acquaintance along to see it. They were all very kind and, like me, probably most impressed by the fact I was on a stage with so many lines and moves learned. I was delighted but in hindsight I can't ever remember any audience members discussing with me my performance or character.

The truth was that beyond knowing lines and moves I hadn't really created a character that audiences really cared about. I'm sure the performance was ok but for those that knew me it was just me spouting some lines I learned rather than them believing in the existence of my character Demetrius.

I did quite a number of shows over the next 15 years, I did a wide variety of roles and when I think about it most were fairly passable. By far my best roles were when I played characters that were exaggerated versions of me.

In terms of successful actors, there are relatively few who are genuinely chameleon like and can successfully play a wide variety of roles convincingly.

Amateur theatre is a great place to develop and hone your presentation style and delivery. It's a great place primarily because you have to put a lot of work into thinking about who your character is. You have to understand what part you play in the story, what your motivations are and ultimately how you will communicate this to an audience given the specific lines that your character has. Weeks of preparation are one of the keys to success.

Preparing your presentation is the key to creating a good and effective experience for you and the people who will be your audience.

Good preparation will make sure you have a real reason why you should be talking to a group of people. And good preparation will give that group of people a reason why they should really listen and respond in a way that achieves your objectives.

Preparing well will make it much easier later on when it comes to you practicing and delivering.

At this stage you will know your objectives and the objectives you want for your audience. You will know your audience, you will know who your primary audience is and who your secondary audience is and you will know what is important to you and what may be important to them.

If you do not know about your audience then you need to talk to, phone or email members of your primary audience and ask them about what they are expecting to get from your presentation.

Ask them what are the key issues and opportunities of the moment and what are some of the most pertinent challenges or factors that they are thinking about.

The less guessing you have to do the better it will be for everyone.

The next thing to do is to decide how important this presentation is to you and therefore how much time are you going to prepare. This is a practical guide to anyone who has other things to do in their lives as well as presentations.

So if your objectives are important then you need to give a good amount of time to plan and practice your presentation.

If they are unimportant, look for the most efficient way to get your preparation done. If you don't know what I mean by this then you need to look back at the chapter on Objectives, all will be explained there.

You have to find your own way, the way that works best for you, but I have always found that little and often helps to create and continually improve a presentation.

I have found this to be much better than just putting large chunks of time by, say for instance an afternoon or a day just ahead of your talk.

In order to maximise success, once you have decided the time you will give to this presentation then put the time in your diary as if it were appointments.

The reason this is so important is because you probably have too much work and not enough time. It is unlikely you will find yourself sitting down thinking I've got nothing to do, what could I do with this time?

You and I know that as well as we plan someone or something is likely to need your time. If for any reason you have to use preparation time for something else, find an alternative time for it. By treating your preparation like an important appointment you will realise that you need to find time elsewhere to make sure it happens.

The sorts of sessions you need to diarise for an important presentation are:

1 Objectives & Audience
2 Outline of Presentation
3 Media & Presentation Space
4 Practice

Step 1 (Objectives & Audience) has been covered in the previous two chapters. In short, know why you are doing it. And know what you want your audience to think, feel and do and know who it is you want to respond in that way.

Step 2 (Outline of Presentation) is about sketching out the outline or story of your presentation. I find it useful to think of what chapters do I need to cover to achieve my objectives and what is the right order to cover these.

You will find the right way for you to build this outline. Some people write a full script, even though they don't learn the script word for word.

Other people will identify the key themes and ideas and trust through knowledge and practice that these will come out right. They then use a series of chapter headings or milestones to establish the key themes and the order.

For instance, I might be doing a presentation on 'Monthly Business Performance'. My structure could be:

Opening Keypoint
Challenges this month
Highlights of the month
Financial report
Forthcoming threats
Forthcoming opportunities
Team performance
Summary
Closing Keypoint

I would then under each structure heading add some keynotes for each section. For instance under challenges I might add; snowy weather, problems with the website, print costs etc.

Once I have all my notes and I know what the strongest messages of that month are, then I will right my summary and opening and closing statements. I do this at the end because having reviewed all the content it is clear to me what my biggest messages are for this presentation.

I often prefer to use this second option because I believe it leads to a more natural performance. There are benefits to using a script particularly when key words or phrases need to be said. The important thing for you is to find the approach that is most useful for you given your situation. In practice I find that although I have a preference for one style, I will use both styles because different speaking activities and audiences make one seem better than the other.

Step 3 (Media & Presentation Space) is when you think about what is the best media to use to communicate this and you should also consider where this presentation is going to happen.

The limits of some rooms mean that you have a more defined choice of what media you can use. You need to think about whether you want to just use Powerpoint or whether you might want video, live drawing or flipcharts or any other appropriate media. Chapter 8 goes into much more detail about the use of media.

The key thing at this stage is to check that the media you want to use is available to you. There is little point putting a lot of time into doing a live internet demonstration if the venue has no Wi-Fi or historically poor and disrupted signals.

It is also a good idea to visit the venue and see the space you are going to be presenting in. If you can think about what is the ideal layout for you then this can increase your success.

Sometimes you can brief someone to set the room up as you want. At other times it is a case of turning up early on the day and setting the room up yourself.

Too many presenters make the mistake of thinking that the room they turn up in is set up in a way they cannot change. If you walk into a room and the chairs and tables are set up in an orderly fashion many people will try and fit into the limitations of that setup.

However, it is better to rearrange that furniture in a way that suits what you want to do and how you think it might work. For example, if openness is a theme you are talking about then move the tables to the back of the room and group the chairs in a semi-circle around you.

I hope you get the idea. If you ask the people who normally organise these rooms they tend to be very open to letting you 'do your thing.'

One other tip is to note how the room smells. In my earlier career I have had to present in rooms that have been damp or smelled of yesterday's lunch.

The downside of these odours is that they can affect the other than conscious mind and the impressions that the audience make of you.

Imagine you are sitting in a room with an unpleasant smell. All you can think of is 'this stinks!' Is that something you would want your audience to connect with you and your presentation?

In my toolkit I always carry room-sprays. There is a science behind the impact of different scents and fragrances. If you are interested do some research and find the fragrance that connects with the mood or feel you are after.

For those of you with a little bit of budget there are smells that can create all sorts of connections for your audience.

A website I like and use a lot is Demeter Fragrance (*demeterfragrance.com* – other sellers are available!). It features an eclectic range of room fragrances. 'Dirt' is great for bringing in a sense of the outdoors, 'Bubble-gum' is very good for getting people to think back to when they were young and 'Popcorn' is excellent for getting people thinking cinematically. They have an enormous range which can really get you thinking about the mood and setting you would like for your audience.

At the very least create a positive environment for your audience. A light spray is normally enough to register something pleasant. However a warning, overpowering the room with these smells can be as bad as doing nothing.

With a little bit of creativity you use smell to enhance the emotional experience for your audience. When you can connect a clear message with a strong emotional response you will create very memorable messages.

The other thing to be aware of is the controllable temperature. If a room is too hot or too cold then this can cause a major distraction for many audiences.

I remember once visiting a presentation room and being very aware of how bitterly cold it was, even on a warm day. The heating in the room was ineffective. I could have accepted that but I knew it would be a constant source of discomfort and irritation for my audience. So on the day of the talk I brought along an electric fan heater, problem solved.

If I had turned up without checking the room then I might not have been able to do anything to change the temperature and it would definitely have impacted negatively on the success of my talk.

Remember all the external factors can have an impact on how you and your message are perceived. Sometimes the extra effort you have put in won't be acknowledged but I can guarantee you that it will have made a difference in the listening and receptiveness of your audience.

Step 4 (Practice) is about putting some time in to practice. Practice is really important because how something sounds out loud is often different from how it sounds when you read it and hear it just in your own head.

As with the other elements of preparation, I would recommend little and often for practice. Your first practice you should try and get as far as you can and make notes of the things that work well and the elements that work less well.

Your memory is strengthened by recall. When you start your other practice sessions you should first recall as much as you can remember from previous sessions. The more you recall the stronger the memory gets.

If you want to know more about memory jump straight to the next chapter, Chapter 4.

In later chapters there are a lot more details about the hows and whys of all these steps that are covered in this chapter.

You can practice on your own. If you are going to do this then audio or video record your practice. Most smartphones, laptops and tablets have recording capabilities. View your practices and do it imagining you are your own coach. Imagine you want the best for the person you are coaching. What would you say to someone that you are trying to help?

It is highly likely you will be more critical of your own performance than anyone else would be. The purpose of review is to identify what works and what doesn't feel right to you. Practice until the presentation feels like a presentation you believe in.

If you want your presentation to be believed, you are the first person you have to convince of the content.

It is also good if you can practice with someone present. If they are not your target audience brief them about who it is you are talking to. Ask for their feedback based around what they would think, feel or do as a result of your presentation. Then compare that with how you would want them to respond.

Get the other person to tell you what worked well. If they have not picked up the key messages that you are trying to communicate then find where it is failing to connect and why. After that you can amend and adjust your presentation.

Very, very few people hit the mark with their presentations without good preparation and practice. Remember we are interested in getting the right results with our audiences!

Dealing With Disaster

If a presentation is important to you then you should always prepare and practice. If you are using other media you should prepare what you would do if there was no laptop, projector or if there were some major power out.

Often in doing this type of disaster prep I have found different ways to present my media which I have actually ended up using in the presentation because it was better than using a more traditional slide deck.

There are no tips or hints, that I am aware of, that are as effective as preparation and practice.

Presenting Boring Subjects:

Some subjects can be considered potentially dry or boring. To minimise this look to present the topic in a way that is meaningful and understandable for your audience. Involvement of the audience is a way to increase both entertainment levels and understanding.

I remember working with an accounts director who had to teach a room of people about profit and loss accounts and balance sheets. This group of people had low interest in mathematics and accounts.

We used a practical example that was meaningful to that audience. We decided to get them to do their own personal accounts. So they thought about their salaries, rents and mortgages, food, transport, clothing and entertaining and used this to construct their own profit and loss accounts.

This made the whole process more interesting and gave more meaning to them. Once they had grasped their personal finances then moving them to business finance was a doddle.

In conclusion get dates in your diary and then take the steps that will prepare you for a great presentation. If it is important then practice, practice and practice.

Action: When you have a presentation or meeting coming up then;

Workout how valuable it is to you, your business or customers and clients.

Put appointments in your diary to think about your objectives, audiences and key messages.

And put appointments in to prepare your message, media and then have time for practice.

Visit the venue and think about room set up.

Video or audio record your practice and review and amend where necessary.

If you can get someone else to rehearse with, brief them about who they are as an audience.

Look for what works in your practice as much as what doesn't.

And finally when diarising I would recommend little and often rather than one big chunk.

Chapter 4
Some Theories on Memory & Being Memorable

In 1885 a German Psychologist called Hermann Ebbinghaus carried out a series of experiments regarding human memory. Over the course of two separate years he used himself as a test subject.

He created nonsense groups of words with multiples of 3 letters so that he was not relying on real words that he may have already encountered in his life up to that date. Nowadays these groups of letters would make great internet passwords because of their difficulty in someone guessing them.

His experiments ranged between 20 minutes and 31 days testing a broad range of times for memory recall. All the results he got allowed him to produce the 'Ebbinghaus Curve of Forgetting.'

He found that not long after a session of learning a lot of information had already been lost. He found that the longer the time went on, the more was lost. But he also discovered that there was a point where a certain amount of information was naturally retained, so not all the information was lost.

In his studies, Ebbinghaus also discovered a few elements that helped us to retain memory.

To be effective in your communication, knowing a little bit about how most of us remember things is a useful bit of knowledge.

If someone stands up and talks to an audience there are a few key elements which will help them to communicate messages that are remembered by the audience.

In any session of learning an audience will remember best:

The start and the finish

Associations

Outstanding elements

Repetition

The **start and the finish** are referred to as the primacy and recency effect. If you think of any film you like, you will probably find it quite easy to remember how the film begins and how it finishes.

The start and finish are ideal times to put in key messages because you already have an advantage. These key points of a presentation are so important that the next chapter is dedicated to thinking more about openings and closings.

Associations are anything that we personally are interested in or we can associate with. If you think about your brain and memory as being a series of files, then you have a variety of files of things that you know or that you are interested in.

It is so much easier to add to a file that already exists than it is to create a completely new file and then add content to it.

Let's imagine you are a fan of the films of Andie McDowell and/or Bill Murray. You are listening to a presentation and the presenter is describing his job as being just like the plot of Groundhog Day.

Because you already have a file with well-formed memories about Groundhog Day then it is quite easy for your brain to tag this new information to that file.

You can easily access your memory of Groundhog Day and it becomes very easy to remember some details of the presenter's job.

For you as the presenter you might know some of the files that will already be in your audiences mind. This way you can connect your important information to subjects that your audience will already have files for.

If you are presenting to sales teams then groups of them may have common interests like skiing, golf, fast cars etc.

In other cases you might not have that knowledge but what you can do is use popular references that are likely to be known by a large number of your audience.

Groundhog Day is a very well-known film, very successful on DVD, often repeated on the television and it is highly likely lots of people have seen it and are familiar with the main part of the plot.

There are plenty of other films, songs, books, people, sporting occasions and many other things that will very likely be well known by large parts of the population. So you have plenty of ideas that you can use to attach your messages to.

It is probably sensible to take a look at your audience and make some good choices about your references.

If you have an audience of 16-18 year olds, talking about Frankie Howard and Up Pompeii might not be the best association for them. In fact you might be Googling Frankie Howard to see what I'm talking about.

OUTSTANDING is about including thoughts and topics that do not appear to belong in your presentation. And then, you associate them with a key thought that you want the audience to remember.

I might talk about there being more chance of seeing the LOCH NESS MONSTER than seeing a brilliant 300 slide Powerpoint presentation.

To emphasise this further I would support this with a picture of the Loch Ness Monster. Because this will be the only time I refer to this and because there is nothing else about mythical beasts in my presentation, then this will be an outstanding reference.

That will increase the chance that if I ask people at the end of my presentation they will be aware of the idea of having too many slides in a presentation.

Repetition increases chances of people remembering. The more we are exposed to an idea the greater the chance that we will remember it.

Repetition can be about repeating the idea when a relevant opportunity arises. So if one of our key messages is about having clear objectives for a presentation, then every time we mention something about objectives we will drop the idea back in.

If you have been following the book up to now, you may have noticed that objectives have been explained in the objectives chapter. It has also been mentioned several times since because I believe it is a really important thing that people take for granted but is at the heart of great, effective presentations. **Repetition** of objectives increases the chance you will remember it.

Another way to use **repetition** is to summarise. When you get to the end of a section of your presentation you can summarise. Summarise the key points only and keep it clear and concise.

So **repetition** is a great idea that gets people to remember.

And if you look back at this section you will see how many times I have used the word **repetition** and put it in bold font to emphasise the impact of **repetition**.

I do this because some people I work with are concerned about repeating themselves. If you are repeating an important point that you want people to remember then keep repeating.

If you are repeating unimportant information, take it out.

The illustration below shows how these techniques can be dropped into a presentation.

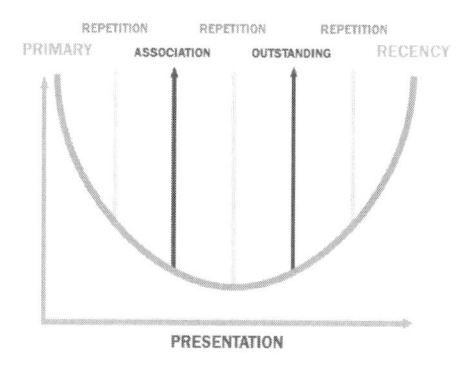

52

To summarise; we know our key messages and to maximise audience recall of those messages we will say them at the start (Primacy) and finish (recency), make them relevant and interesting to your audience by using their associations, we will use outstanding stories, anecdotes or images to associate the key points with and we will be repeating them through the presentation and use summaries to reinforce memorable messages.

That covers some ways to make your presentation memorable. What about how you are able to remember your own presentation.

This method is very good for remembering the order of your presentation without having to use written notes.

This is a version of a method that I learned from Dominic O'Brien, a man who has been world memory champion on numerous occasions. Since then a number of other people have written good books on this subject but I still like and use Dominic's methods. I have put some details in the further reading section at the back of the book.

I include this technique because I have found it to be the most effective and the easiest to apply to a number of memory challenges. This technique involves Location, Imagination and Association.

First think of a regular journey that you make. This is the location element. The easiest one for me is the order that I most often would go through my house. My journey goes like this:

In the morning I wake in the bedroom

I go onto the <u>landing</u>

Then into the <u>office</u>

Then next the <u>bathroom</u>

Down the <u>stairs</u>

Then into the <u>dining room</u>

I would next go into the <u>kitchen</u>

Then into my <u>utility room</u>

Then the <u>downstairs bathroom</u>

And finally into the <u>living room</u>.

This journey would be the way I remember all the rooms in my house. This journey is known so well to me that I do not have any problem recalling the rooms in this order.

However before I created it for this purpose it was a journey I had not thought about. This journey gives me 10 places to associate memories with.

Journeys can involve any places or landmarks you encounter when you think about it.

I have a journey with 45 landmarks to remember the Presidents of the USA in order. I know there have only been 44 Presidents but Grover Cleveland served 2 different terms.

I have a 52 location journey which is a journey to a previous place of work. The journey is about 6 miles and the landmarks are such things as traffic lights, pubs, distinctive houses and roundabouts. More about that journey later.

There are plenty of journeys that you already know. As well as places of work, there are journeys to friends, family, sporting venues and others. All of them will have unique landmarks that allow you to create opportunities for learning massive amounts of information.

The great thing about this technique is that it will work on journeys that you just invent in your own minds. You have not been round to my house yet you can easily picture the journey on the previous page.

Having created the journey you should test by recalling the journey in order a couple of times to confirm that you have the right order. When I use this technique I always see it as if I am seeing it through my own eyes, rather than imagining that I can see me doing this journey. It does make a big difference.

The next task is to visualise a word in the individual room settings. To make this work the visualisation needs to be exaggerated (remember 'outstanding' from the memory presentation). This is the imagination part of the technique.

Practice using this list below

1) Wallet
2) Snake
3) Screwdriver
4) Peach
5) Drum
6) Hat
7) Piano
8) Goat
9) Mirror
10) Tank

Typically if I gave this list out to a group of people and ask them to tell me the words back in the order I gave them out most would struggle to get to 3 words in the right order.

The good thing is that they will nearly always remember the first and last word, proving the primacy and recency effect.

So if now is a good time for you to do some practice read through the instructions with me and start using your imagination.

In our journey I would imagine waking up in my bedroom and seeing a huge wallet, stuffed with colourful banknotes sitting on the end of my bed. This would be a wallet that I would most associate with. The wallet I have is a black leather wallet that smells as we know leather smells. It would be the style that you would think of first. This is the Association element. I use the ideas that most easily come to mind when I think of a word or an idea (My descriptions here will be occasionally vague because your experience means that you will associate with a different type of object.).

Then I would imagine a huge snake on my landing. The snake in this case is a character that was created at Adams called Jake the Snake. It is a large friendly snake green in colour with a red zigzag pattern running through its body.

When I get into my office there would be an enormous red plastic handled screwdriver on the floor. I would imagine turning it to screw a large Philips screw into the wall. As I turn the screw I see brickdust dropping onto my office floor.

As I walk into the bathroom there would be a giant peach with a big bite taken out of it, I would see the juice running down the side and the stone would be visible. And I can smell the peach.

Then on the stairs there would be a large <u>drum</u>. This would be the sort of drum used in military marching bands. I would imagine playing it so that I could hear the drum but also I could feel the vibration of the drum as I hit it. The beat playing on the drum is the first one that comes to mind for you.

Next I would imagine the dining room and there would be a big top <u>hat</u>. The hat would have felt ribbon around it and it would also have white rabbits sitting in it, like a magician's top hat.

I would then move to the kitchen. And in the kitchen would be a large black grand <u>piano</u>. The piano would be playing a piece of music. The piece of music playing is the first piece of piano music that comes to your mind. Hear it playing clearly and imagine the keys moving on the piano as it is playing independently.

Moving into the utility room there would be a large white <u>goat</u> tethered to the washing machine, eating my clothes and towels and making the occasional bleating sound. You can also hear the sound of its hooves as it shuffles around the wooden floor.

Next to the downstairs bathroom. Here there would be a massive <u>mirror</u>. The mirror would go from floor to ceiling and to make it extra memorable I would imagine the mirror smashing into pieces. You can hear the sound of the mirror as it comes crashing to the floor. If you see it in slow motion that will make it even more stand out.

And then as I walk into the living room there is a big <u>tank</u>. In my imagination it is a large German Tiger tank from World War 2. Choose the tank that comes to mind for you. The tank would be turning and churning up the carpet. There would be the sound and smell of its diesel engine and it would fire its gun.

You can now go back to my journey and although you have not been to my house, you can imagine what that journey might look like.

Start at the first room. Think what the first room was remember the activity in the room and name the word. Go through each room and order and see if you can recall the word from each location.

If you have given these pages your full attention for a couple of minutes you should find that you can remember the words.

Have a go now.

If it is not working for you go back and make the visualisation more of a sensory experience. Add more sounds, movement, tastes and smells.

For instance, if you cannot remember the wallet, imagine all the banknotes and coins falling out and imagine the noise of cascading coins falling on the floor.

The more outstanding you make these visualisations and the more senses you engage, the better these ideas will lodge in your memory.

Try this exercise for yourself. As soon as you have assigned a visualisation to each word on your journey then write down the words in the right order and compare them with the right answers. Then ten minutes later try writing the words again in the right order. If you have remembered the words doing this, you will find that anytime over the next few days you will be able to recall the list.

Before you go to bed at night you will think of the list and you will be able to remember them clearly. When you get up the next morning you will be able to remember the list. The more you recall the list the stronger the memory gets and the longer it will last. You will be amazed how well this works!

How Does This Help With Learning A Presentation?

I will assume that when you are creating your excellent presentation you are going to be talking about things that you have knowledge about.

When we have a lot of knowledge about a subject we can probably talk about it for a long time and we are also very capable of digressing into lots of different areas and loosely connected avenues.

To make sure our presentation is focussed and that the messages are delivered effectively it would make sense for our presentation to be presented in a logical order and sticking to the specific areas we would want to talk about.

Let's say I am planning a presentation on editing music files. It is a huge area and there are all sorts of angles that I could cover.

For the benefit of this example I am talking to an audience of people who want a basic idea of what you can do and what is out there.

If I were to break my talk into chapters they could be;

What is music <u>editing</u>?

What <u>kit</u> do you need?

What <u>software</u> is available?

<u>Mixing</u> music files

<u>Creating</u> your own music

<u>Burning</u> to CD

<u>Converting to MP3</u>

A practical <u>example</u>

Next steps

<u>Q&A</u>

I'm going to use another journey just in case you want to practice this with me. If you wanted to use the first journey I gave you then you can overwrite that journey with new information.

The more you recall the new information the quicker it replaces what was previously there.

So my new journey is the journey around a 'Cluedo' board.

A cluedo board is a flat two dimensional board of minimal design. To bring the board to life I use my imagination to bring life into the rooms. The Hall for me would be a large room with animal trophies on the wall and suits of armour along the side. The lounge would be full of large leather sofas and a huge roaring fireplace, the dining room would feature a dining table large enough to seat twenty people. All the time I am engaging my imagination the easier it is to recall these things.

So to remember my ten topics for my editing music file speech I would do the following. The first is to memorise the journey around the cluedo board.

We start at the centre **"Clue" starting space**

Then the **Hall** and going clockwise

Lounge

Dining Room

Kitchen

Ballroom

Conservatory

Billiards Room

Library

And **Study**

That gives us 10 locations.

All the words underlined on the chapter list on the previous page are the keywords that would prompt me about what topic I am talking about.

So let's start to learn these words.

Starting at the 'Clue Starting Space' my first word is '<u>editing</u>'.

Here I would imagine Rik Mayall and Adrian Edmonsen from the BBC slapstick comedy series 'Bottom'.

Rik would have a frying pan in his hand and would be smacking Adrian continually over the head. Head hitting = 'Ed 'Iting.

This action uses OUTSTANDING to make it memorable. If I just imagined someone sitting in that space doing some editing it might work but the slapstick one makes it more outstanding.

This approach is also good for longer or more technical words that don't immediately create pictures. Changing a word like 'editing' into 'Head-hitting' makes it easier to animate in your imagination.

Then in the Hall we want the word **kit**.

So in the Hall the car KITT from the television series Knightrider would be revving up. The red lights on the front of the car scrolling from left to right.

In the lounge I need to remember the word **software**. I would imagine trying on a beautiful soft coat and running my hand up and down the sleeve, feeling how soft the fabric is.

62

In the dining room the word is **mixing**. Here I would imagine a cement mixer on the dining table. I would imagine shovelling cement into the mixer and the noise of the mixer as it revolves.

In the kitchen the next word is **creating**. Here I would imagine making bodybuilder protein shakes (creatine). Bodybuilders would be there with their big plastic cups and straws waiting in a line for their protein shakes.

In the Ballroom I want to remember **burning**. In the middle of the floor I would have a massive bonfire. I would sense the heat and hear the crackle of this fire.

Then in the Conservatory we have **Converting to MP3**. Here I would have rugby posts in front of me and I would imagine kicking 3 Military Policemen over the posts. For those of you who are not familiar with rugby, kicking over the post is called a conversion. So in this case I am converting 3 MPs, so I hope you can see how that works in terms of memorising.

In the Billiards room we have the word **example**. Here I would have a very full man sitting at a table looking ill and surrounded by loads of fried eggs; eggs ample!

Then in the Library the word is **next steps**. So here in the library I would have big stone steps that lead up to a Next clothing store. The store would have the big Next signage above the door.

Finally in the study I need to remember **Q&A**. Here I would imagine a long queue of people all being buried under hay that is falling from the sky; Queue and Hay!

The great thing is once I have learned these chapters at no point am I distracted by thoughts of what comes next. The next chapter heading will be there in my head when I need it. I know not to meander into other topics because I have the confidence just to focus on the chapter I need to talk about now.

This knowledge makes me feel very comfortable with my presentation and allows me to be focussed with my audience concentrating on being present with them and not trying to think 'what on earth comes next!'.

The more you practice this the easier it gets for you to stretch your imagination. I hope I have shown you how pushing the formation of those words creates unusual and outstanding images. You will soon realise just how memorable those images can be.

It might seem difficult at first. Remember for a number of you this is a skill you don't use very much so it might take a few goes to click with you. I guarantee you that if you put the practice in you will have a system that will work for you again and again and again.

Now would be a good time to practice this. Find something that you would like to learn, create the appropriate size journey and engage your imagination.

I have created a range of journeys that I have written down or created excel files to save them. I find that spreadsheets work well for this but you could use any sort of word processing file or you could keep written journals of journeys and information remembered.

So in this chapter we have learned that information will be forgotten over time if we do not recall it. We know that there are ways for an audience to remember better if we make use of the start and the finish (the Primacy and Recency effect), if we use Associations, if we include elements that are Outstanding and if we use Repetition, Repetition and Repetition.

There is also the Location/Association/Imagination method for memorising key information in the order we want to talk about it.

Action: Memorise the ways that we can impact audience memory

Learn the journey memory technique

Create your own journeys

Find a presentation or some information you want to remember

Practice turning them into animations

Practice breaking difficult words down

Chapter 5
Opening & Closing a Presentation

How you start a presentation is vitally important for your success.

It is vitally important for your audience that you say something that gets their attention and gives you a good start that helps to manage your confidence, nerves and focus.

Equally how you finish is incredibly important because it is that point of how do you leave your audience and what do they now do as a result of your presentation. And remember the power of the 'primacy and recency effect' in helping your audience to remember.

The majority of the content in this chapter will focus on connected opening and closing. This is because if you are clear about your audience and clear about your objectives, your main messages should also be clear. A connected opening and closing is a fantastic way to cement your ideas into the minds of your audience.

Before we do that there is one area that I want to talk about. Introducing yourself. Let me remind you why audiences are present. Firstly they are there for themselves. Secondly they are there because of who you are, what you have to say or because they need to learn something for their benefit.

If you are David Beckham, Angelina Jolie, Lewis Hamilton or Lady Gaga, introducing yourself and telling us something more about you that we didn't know is wonderful. If you are a great inventor you can say I'm Martin Cooper and I invented the handheld mobile phone. That will get people's attention because whilst the name might not be so well known the invention certainly is.

However most of us are accountants, teachers, trainers, marketeers, salespeople, managers, directors, students or supervisors. We mostly do not qualify for the part that says the audience have come along because of who we are. They are here for what we have to say or what they need to learn.

My advice to you is do not open with your name, job and a brief CV. Most of your audience don't care.

Think about how many talks you have listened to. How often are you turned off by a talk that starts "Hi I'm Bill Blahblah, I am head of Blahblah. I use to work at Not Interested Design, I moved onto boring.com and then I was head of zilch at the Tedious Agency."

Or there is a favourite bugbear of mine "For those that don't know me I'm……..''

Does that mean for those that do know you, you are somebody else?

Your audience don't care! For some of them you have missed your first chance to make a connection and you have given yourself an uphill struggle to make that connection. You have also wasted the primacy opportunity.

Your name and your work experience could have a lot of value. So don't throw that value away by listing your CV. If you want to use your experiences to good effect and make good connections with your audience then that will be covered later in the storytelling chapter.

If you just want to communicate who you are and what you do, either introduce yourself after you have introduced your topic. And make your own introduction brief. Or put your name and job title on your first slide and let that sort it out.

Don't even start with hello, good morning, good afternoon or any other welcome. If you are one of a number of speakers your audience are saying "Get on with it!"

This can all seem a little harsh. But I'm assuming if you've made it this far into this book you are serious about being a more effective presenter. My challenge to you is:

Do a presentation that makes your audience want to come and find you later on and find out who you are.

Wouldn't that be great? You have put a lot of work in, you've delivered a great presentation. A presentation that you really enjoyed delivering. And at the end of it members of your primary audience are seeking you out because you made a real connection with them.

The second major re-occurring presentation turnoff is the issue of the old saying *"Tell them what you are going to tell them, tell them and then tell them what you told them."*

If applied properly I believe this is a really good rule. However, I am often presented with an agenda as an example of tell them what you are going to tell them.

And a list of topics at the end of a presentation as a tell them what you told them.

My belief about this statement is that the tell them refers to your key message or messages.

These are the things that if you stopped anybody at the door at your presentation and asked them "what are the main messages of my presentation?" the things that they would tell you would be exactly what you were trying to communicate.

For example, if I were talking to retail managers about how to make customers comfortable in their stores, I might open my presentation by showing them a video of people smiling, making eye contact and saying hello.

I would then take them through why that makes people more comfortable to shop and how it makes it easier for those customers to approach staff when they are have questions.

I would summarise and finish with the video because that is what I want them to take away and do and that's what I want them to communicate to their staff.

There is no need for an agenda, all I'm interested in is that the audience take a message away that will make the experience more pleasurable for their customers and will probably facilitate more sales and repeat visits.

I have lots of other ideas about retail but I do not have the necessary inspiration to write a book, if you like that sort of thing read the work of Paco Underhill.

Sorry that was another digression, that's one of the problems of writing in the conversational style!

Now let me continue with how you go about opening and closing a presentation. There are many different ways that you can open and close a presentation. The selections below give you a range of different options and cover a number of different usages.

The ideas I will focus on are:

Stories & historical events
Key memorable or learning points
Questions
Quotes

Jokes
Statistics
Shock, surprise or contradiction
Creating an imagined future
WiiFM
Nested Loops

Stories/Historical Events

Stories are a way to connect with people and are good for setting up an alternative context for a difficult subject. Chapter 10 covers storytelling in a lot more detail.

Key Memorable Point

Starting your presentation with one of the key things you want your audience to remember is very powerful.

It starts the presentation with a focus that you want your audience to have and has their mind in the place you want it to be from the very beginning.

The great thing about this is that your opening statement can be a real 'wow' statement;

"If you follow the technique I am going to show you, you will triple your income over the next year!"

A statement like that at the start of a presentation is likely to get a number of people to sit up and take notice.

You would then elaborate and prove your point, if proof were necessary. Your finish would match the opening with the possible addition of a challenge;

"If you follow the technique I have shown you, you will triple your income over the next year. So when are you going to start to take action!"

Using this process is very effective. If you use this with genuine self-belief it will make a big impact with audiences.

Questions

Every time you ask a question your audience have to answer it. Whether it's out loud or in their head. It's true isn't it? If you just answered "Yes" the point is proved. If you just answered "No" the point is also proved. Using questions is a good attention grabber that puts your audiences headspace in a place where you want it.

Always pause for one or two beats to allow time for the question to be answered.

If you finish on the same question that you started with, you might deliver it with a different inflection.

For example, you might start with *"How good a presenter do you want to be?"* It would be asked as an open, light question for your audience to consider.

Having then done a presentation that informs your audience of ways and means to be a better presenter the question *"How good a presenter do you want to be?"* might be delivered much more as an inspiring challenge.

Quotes

A good quote that clearly supports your key message makes a great start. I would always suggest you use less obvious quotes because that will demonstrate a level of intelligence to your audience that will be useful.

When you use more obscure quotes briefly explain who that person was or is. The incredible internet and, of course, the wonderful world of books are full of inspiring quotes.

One I came across recently but have not yet used is a quote from a book by the author Kenko, a 14th century Buddhist monk from Japan from his book A Cup of Sake Beneath The Cherry Trees. The quote reads;

"It is a most wonderful comfort to sit alone beneath a lamp, book spread before you, and commune with someone from the past whom you have never met."

I am sure you can think of many opportunities to start a presentation with a warm and rich quote like that.

I tend to collect good quotes because searching around for them at the last minute tends to be more stressful than it needs to be.

About 15 years ago I did a really enjoyable market research project for a greetings card company. I got to talk to people who really cared about the cards they bought and so would make a point of regularly dropping into card shops and buying cards for people when they thought the card was highly appropriate for them. Even if their birthdays were months away.

I was always one of those people that noticed it was a friend or family members birthday in the next couple of days, so I went looking for a card and got the best that was available. The cards mostly failed to be really appreciated because they didn't really reflect the other person's character or interests or it didn't illustrate the relationship between them and me. This was very typical behaviour for one of the 95%, the away motivated.

However, through the great insight of these card buyers I changed my habit and bought a card because it was right for someone and not because it was their birthday today.

I also found a draw just for these cards because that made them easy to find when I needed them. As a result many people praise me for my birthday card choices.

When it comes to finding quotes the same is true. When I hear a quote I really like, I will add it to a word file I keep and so when I feel a presentation needs a quote I have a healthy stock of highly appropriate quotes. It removes a lot of stress and can enhance a presentation significantly.

If the quote is obscure I will also research the author of the quote and record some interesting or relevant facts.

If you are going to use an oft used quote try and add something new for your audience. If you research quotes sometimes there is an extra piece that your audience may not be aware of.

For instance some of you may be familiar with the phrase 'There's no such thing as a free lunch.' This is known as Friedman's Law after the economist Milton Friedman and was the title of a book in 1975. However, the phrase was used notably by a number of different people before that.

So this quote rather than just making a point about the lack of free lunches could be the opener about how to be the one to get the credit despite not being the originator of an idea, product or service.

Jokes

Jokes can work very well but they are also a risky opening. Get your joke or your audience wrong and your start can fall flat. It can be more difficult to recover if your joke takes a dive.

The other risk with jokes is that it goes really well, people remember it but it has no link to your key messages. The result is joke remembered, messages not.

One speaker I knew was very funny and had all you needed to tell great jokes. He did a presentation that was incredibly funny and that was a big hit with his audience.

The next year he approached me and said "I'm not sure I'm going to do jokes this year. My message last year was about the great opportunity we had to increase sales of accessories. Last year our sales went backwards, I think my message got lost."

When jokes work well they are delivered to support the key message of the speaker and tend to demonstrate a level of intelligence in the speaker.

Jokes tend to work best when they are used as an outstanding moment within a presentation, again as long as they are linked to a key message.

If you use other people's jokes then credit them like you would credit a quote. Comedians have put a lot of time into producing these jokes. You wouldn't hesitate to credit a business leader or author so do something nice for a comedian.

Statistics

Good statistics, like good questions, are great at grabbing people's attention. Statistics are especially good when they shock or surprise an audience.

Having worked in market research for such a long time I know that statistics are a very flexible commodity. No single statistic is either bad news or good news. A good statistician can make them say what they want them to say.

They make great headlines and the body of a presentation can be used to explain the context and assumptions but you will likely have your audience listening to you because your opening statistic grabbed their attention.

To make a bigger impact, if you are using Powerpoint or flipcharts you can have the figures written as large as you can. This adds emphasis to any verbal messages you are making.

"LinkedIn launched in May 2003, at the end of the first month it had 4,500 members. It currently has 347,000,000 members worldwide"

Again a quote like the one above gives you a number of directions that you can go in. You can talk about how the world is much more connected these days, you can talk about how phenomenal growth can be achieved and I am sure you can also choose a whole host of other connecting ideas from that single statistic.

Shock, Surprise & Contradiction

Surprising people at the start of the presentation is a great way to grab their attention and open their mind.

Sometimes saying the opposite of what your argument or idea is will work well. You will then use the rest of your presentation to disprove your opening and by doing so take your audience with you as to why your idea is great.

The reason this technique is so effective is because often people are in their own heads thinking about all sorts of different things they have done, haven't done or need to do. A good shock opening snaps them out of their heads and brings them very quickly into the present.

This is one you can have a lot of fun practicing with because the best ones have a good level of dramatic performance with them.

A good one I heard was at a neighbourhood watch meeting.

The meeting was about getting people involved. This was in an area that seemed very peaceful. Before the talk I spoke to a few people. They were happily sipping tea and coffee and helping themselves to the nice selection of biscuits.

When I asked them why they were here most said they had turned up to be polite to the organiser but that they had little or no interest.

The presenter stood up and said "I am going to tell you how easily I can steal from the houses in this area because I am a professional house burglar."

This was not what they were expecting to hear. He had the full attention of the room and had raised their interest significantly by the end.

Be careful with this type of opening but when you get it right it can be brilliant.

Creating An Imagined Future

In this opening you present a future (6 months, a year, 5 years…) where you describe the ideal outcome in rich detail.

You could talk to them about working for a company that is loved by its customers, doing a job that gets them leaping out of bed in the morning to do. A job that pays them the money that allows them to have the life they want.

In this opening you are attempting to put their minds in a place of success and positivity that opens their minds to any possibility that will get them to actually live that experience.

You give your audience the chance to consider this positive experience and you then use your presentation to show them how to get there.

You can also present a negative experience which would be where they could be if they do not follow your ideas. The benefit of this approach is that this is the type that is often good to inspire the 95%, the away motivated.

Painting a negative picture is a way of bringing potential pain to someone where that pain does not currently exist in their minds.

This type of introduction can be the basis to inspire some change from someone who is very happy with how things are now and who ordinarily will see no reason to adapt the way they work.

The cosmetics industry is fantastic at doing this. They have created a whole range of problems that we didn't know we had and luckily for them they also have the solution.

There was a time when most people had no idea that cellulite was a problem. The cosmetics industry informed people it was and then they described their solution and how it worked. Now the whole world knows. Very neat!

If you are going to paint a negative picture it can be very effective. It needs a middle and an end that also offers a clear direction to hope. That is of course if you want the group to feel positive.

Clearly there are some occasions where you might want them to carry some doubts and concerns because that is what is going to give them the inspiration to achieve.

WiiFM

Whenever you are in an audience listening to the speaker you will ask yourself the question 'What's in it For Me?' This creates the acronym WiiFM.

As a presenter answering this question can create brilliant openings and closings.

"In the next 20 minutes I am going to show you how you can get that promotion a year ahead of schedule."

I'm standing here talking to you today because I am going to tell you the answer to your money problems."

Looking at the quotes above one opener is a toward motivation, one is an away. Both straight away answer the question of what is in it for you. If either of those things were why you were here I would think I would have got your attention from the start.

This type of presentation then includes the hows and whys in the middle. It would then finish reminding the audience of the benefits.

Make sure that you are confident about your claim and don't underestimate the ability of your audience to see through your passion and enthusiasm. I once heard of a business leader pitching an idea to a supplier. With gusto he said "If you half your prices I will double your sales."

Within a couple of seconds the astute supplier said "So you want me to work twice as hard for the same money!"

Make your opener genuinely attractive for your audience and again this will pay off for you.

Nested Loop

I have left this until last in this section because this is a technique that is under-utilised. But it is under-utilised because it takes quite a lot of work to prepare it and it definitely benefits from good practice.

The nested loop is a term to describe a story that has a number of stories within it. It is like a Russian Doll of stories.

The idea is you start to tell a story, then at a certain point you stop and start to tell a second story. Part way through that story you stop and you begin a third story. Each time you stop the audience wants more because the story is incomplete. It appears you have left them unfulfilled.

You continue with and complete the third story, then you complete the end of the second story and then you complete the story you opened with.

There are some stand-up comedians who use this technique particularly well. The first one I was aware of was Harry Hill. He has a quick fire delivery that would start with something, appear to go off at a tangent and then appear to go off at another tangent. In his act he did this about seven or eight times.

Later on he then went back and closed off each element in reverse order. It was fantastic. I often think that a lot of stand-ups do not get enough credit for their craft. Lots of people can tell jokes but really good stand-ups understand the effects that this style of performance has on an audience.

The beauty of this technique is in understanding how our unconscious mind works.

If you give yourself a question that you can't answer immediately, your brain carries on trying to answer it.

We have all had the experience of trying really hard to remember something or someone. We rack our brains but whilst the answer appears to be on the tip of our tongue it just won't come out. At a point we give up, we can't find it. Then later on to our surprise the answer just pops into our head.

Not just that but it is usually accompanied by a nice pleasurable feeling. Sometimes it's a 'Eureka feeling,' or sometimes that feeling is just a sense of relief. Whatever it is, it is a very nice feeling.

The nested loop does a job on a couple of levels. First of all because it leaves answers incomplete for the audience they tend to be a little more focussed on what is going on. We don't like things that are not resolved.

When the loop is closed and each story is finished it not only brings relief and nice feelings to your audience, it tends to also create a number of outstanding memorable moments for your audience as each loop is completed.

Close the loop with a key point and you have very likely created another strong memory for your audience.

It is a great technique and if you have seen or heard this technique done well you will remember that experience.

This is quite an advanced technique so practice is really important.

Rule of 3

One element more related to opening and closing summaries is considering the rule of 3. This means that your open or close consists of 3 key-message or 3 word statements.

Many psychologists believe that we can successfully hold between 5 and 9 thoughts in our short term memory at any time. That's why people who put 20 to 30 messages in their presentation are likely to leave a room of 100s with mixed messages. It's just too much to remember.

3 is a good number of messages that most people can comfortably remember and it can create a discipline in a speaker to prioritise messages to deliver more effective and consistent take-out messages.

Let me give you some examples that you might be familiar with;

"Life, liberty and the pursuit of happiness"
    Thomas Jefferson, US Declaration of Independence

"Education, education, education"
                            Tony Blair

"Never before in the field of human conflict was so much owed by so many, to so few"
                            Winston Churchill

And I particularly like the next one because of the number of repeating threes it uses;

"Today we are introducing three revolutionary products, a widescreen iPod with touch controls, a revolutionary mobile phone and the third is a breakthrough internet communications device.

So three things, a widescreen iPod with touch controls, a revolutionary mobile phone and a breakthrough internet communications device.

An iPod, a phone and an internet communicator.

An iPod, a phone and an internet communicator.

Are you getting it?

These are not three separate devices, this is one device and we are calling it iPhone."

Steve Jobs

There is something very compelling about the rule of 3 and I would argue that for the listener these statements not only make it easier to be remembered but actually are pleasurable to listen to. So try some of your rules of 3.

Thank You

One of the things that came up again and again when I interviewed audience members at conference events was the question of applause.

Most reasonable people, and there are a lot of them out there, would prefer to applaud after someone has given a speech, particularly a good speech. However in mass audiences people are unsure of etiquette and behaviour. They tend to look around at what everyone else is doing and follow the majority.

Often if there is hesitation then a speaker might well not get applause for their presentation. If the first speaker does not get applause that will usually mean that the behaviour has been set and no one else who comes up will get applause either.

This phenomenon is covered in a brilliant book by Robert Cialdini called "Influence: Science and Practice". He has termed this 'Social Proof'. If you have not read this book then seek it out, for me it is the foundation of influence.

Social proof reflects the way large groups of people make decisions by looking to others about how they should respond in what are usually situations of uncertainty.

When I work with a company for the first time at their conference I ask them if their audiences applaud. About half will say no. My next question is then "Would you like them to applaud?" With a short pause for humility, the answer is often "Yes".

In order to get applause there are two things you should do.

The first is before the event ask a couple of people in the audience to applaud with gusto when your presentation is finished. If they applaud without reservation, the behaviour is clear for everyone else and then they too applaud. This has worked every time so far.

If the applause is done with a little uncertainty it is less successful, so always with gusto. Once the first presenter has had applause the behaviour is set and the others will get their applause too.

There are a few reasons applause is important. Firstly from my interviews most audience members would like to show their appreciation for the effort and time that the speaker has put in on their behalf.

A second reason is that if one of the objectives of your conference event is to make your audience feel good about being connected with your business, a day of applause makes most audience members feel like they have been to a good day.

A third reason is it is a good reward for the speaker. It is a thank you for the time and effort and it is often intoxicating and will make a speaker want to get more. An incentive for many to do good work when it comes to future presentations.

So getting people to start to applaud was the first thing. The second thing is for you to say "Thank you" at the very end of your presentation. Your audience will need a clear signal to know your presentation has finished and to date there is no better way than saying "Thank you". Polite and clear.

These two clear thoughts around applause can make a massive difference to the effectiveness and the feedback of your presentations and events.

All these techniques for opening and closing are just a small selection of the many ways to begin and end your presentation. This selection gives you a wide variety to use which is useful if you present regularly to the same audience and you are looking to give them variety.

To summarise; opening and closing are really valuable.

Putting emphasis on how you do this will often pay off handsomely. I have made you aware of a small selection there are plenty more ways to open and close. Try some of them and you will find that they make a big difference to how well you can engage an audience.

Actions:

Consider using a variety of different openings and closings for your presentations

Collect good quotes

Research good quotes to see if there are other useful stories behind the quote

Prime an audience for applause if it is a suitable audience for applause

Chapter 6
Making a Connection

When it really matters, you are going to put a lot of work and effort into your presentations. Remember you and I are doing all this for a reason. We are looking to get results! Moreover we are looking to get good effective results.

If you are going to get the results you want then you need to know that the audience need to buy you before they buy your message.

There are statistics everywhere that talk about how quickly people make their minds up about new people they meet. Lots of figures are quoted, whether its 10 seconds, 15 seconds or 20 seconds, the one thing that is certain is that it is very quick!

Think about the last person you met for the first time. If after 20 seconds I asked you the question "well, what do you think of him/her", the vast majority of you would be able to give me a reasonable answer as to whether you think the person is nice, nasty, untrustworthy, boring, charismatic or whatever descriptor was appropriate.

Only a small number of people would say they would need more time to form any opinion.

This phenomenon is present in many areas of our lives and has a massive impact on how we listen and what we hear. It stands to reason that when it's our turn to present our idea or view, then we want to make a connection with our audience so that they really listen.

Making a connection is often about demonstrating to your audience that in some way you are, or you think, a little bit like them. It helps to have some common ground.

There are clearly cases where setting yourself up as being completely different to your audience may be important. This may be because you are speaking to them because you are different and you want them to be clear about that. And the reason you are there talking to them is they have a real need for difference.

Even in cases like this, making some sort of connection so they will listen to you is valuable. It is extremely rare for a successful presenter to get up in front of an audience and want to make no connection with them and yet still manage to successfully communicate their message to that audience.

There are a variety of ways that you can use to make that connection.

First we will assume that this is an audience that you know and that know you.

There are simple everyday things that will connect you with your audience. There might be types of meetings that you all attend. There might be particular processes that you have to go through in your work.

It could be that you know there are a high proportion of your audience that have families. There are so many different work and social commonalities for you to choose from.

Every time you talk about these elements you are giving yourself a chance to make a connection. The thing to be aware of is the potential impact of that connection.

If you introduce the idea of a great holiday, chances are more people will be in a more positive place in their mind. Mention a particularly painful work inspection and you may get the opposite response.

The most important thing with making the connection is relaxing the audience to feel that you are like them or think like them. If you can achieve this you increase the chances of them really listening to you because it tends to relax their critical factor.

The critical factor in this instance is the way an audience member reacts to you and your subject.

If you are anti genetically modified (GM) foods and someone you don't know stands up in front of you and starts talking about the benefits of GM foods then it has an impact on how you listen and what you hear.

The tendency is that anything you do not agree with, you will dismiss it as rubbish and not properly listen to the arguments that are connected with it. The only things you will really hear are any of the downsides of GM food. And these will only reinforce your already strong views.

The benefit of making a connection is that the speaker can relax the critical factor. Where somebody has started their presentation and made a connection that makes you feel they are a little like you, you are more likely to listen better and hear what the arguments are before making your mind up.

So if our GM presenter has made you think that he or she is a little like you in some way, then you will at least be prepared to listen to their arguments and give them a fairer hearing.

They may say something like;

"I am someone who is very concerned about the food that me and my family are eating. I am also concerned with how the growing, farming and manufacture of food can have an impact on our environment."

This way the speaker is looking to match the views of the audience before they introduce the idea of GM foods.

But making a connection on its own does not win the argument.

As the presenter, if you are going to change someone's mind you still need to have very good arguments to counter their objections.

Not making a connection will make your job considerably more difficult.

Making that connection is very important and if you know your audience may be hostile to your ideas, then always think about how you can make a connection before presenting your facts. It will increase their openness to you and your ideas and arguments.

No matter how strong you believe your thoughts or ideas are, making a connection is a vital part of being heard. You will be aware of your everyday conversation and the difference you have in communicating with someone to whom you have a connection versus the experience of communicating with someone you don't. The difference is huge.

With those you know well you are better able to hear their ideas because you are comfortable with them. Other people who you know but have no connection with will get a different response from you.

If someone like that approaches you there is more chance that you will be wary and on-guard.

If you are not well known to the audience you need to give them the information they need to know that tells them you are like them or think like them in some way.

This is where really good research of your audience will pay off. The research will give you numerous opportunities to find some common ground with your audience that will have them unconsciously lowering their critical factors and listening to you.

Have you ever had the experience of being at an airport, a bar or a coffee shop and someone you have never met opens a conversation with you. Most people's initial response is to be irritated by the intrusion. However the chatty someone then talks about where they are from and that's your home town! Or they say which sports team they support and that's your team!

Within a few minutes you are comfortably chatting with this person and you welcome their company. By the time you go your separate ways you have been happily chatting for an hour or more!

You get the idea. And if you think hard enough you will remember an occasion when this has happened to you.

This process goes on at many a presentation and so creating that connection is a job well worth doing.

In practice what this means is that you weave into your introduction common thoughts and experiences that allow them to get who you are. An extension of this idea is in the Storytelling chapter later on.

Or if you want to try some practice why not be the person at the airport, bar or coffee shop that initiates a conversation with a complete stranger.

Communicating Clearly:

In normal conversation you will hear people often using the negative way to describe situations and needs. For example:

Using negatives does not make the task of influence impossible but it does make it more challenging.

However I could have written;

Using positives will greatly assist the process of influencing.

Say both statements to yourself and note the emotional reaction you get, then think how your audience might react to both. Think about which one is best understood. Which one did you understand the easiest when you read it?

Many psychologists theorise that historically our brain was primarily designed for survival rather than really living. This means that our senses are on the lookout for danger constantly.

For most of us, the way our brains are wired means we find it much easier to say what we don't want rather than what we do.

The best everyday examples are parents communicating with children. "Don't spill the milk", "Don't run away" and "Don't bang that door" These are some common instructions you will have heard very often if you are a parent yourself or if you spend time around parents and children.

You will probably also be aware that those instructions are often followed by spilt milk, running and banging doors! The problem is in order to process it you have to put the idea you don't want into someone's head and then they have to negate it.

Parents and teachers I know have all talked about a significant difference in response when they say the positive instruction. They more often get the results they want.

Ask children to 'hold the cup carefully', 'stay with me' or 'close the door gently' and you might be surprised by getting better results more often.

Children offer the best examples of this but it is also extremely common in adults.

A story I remember, when researching an audience, was about an annual conference at an engineering firm. The firm had had a very successful year and at the conference the CEO was going to announce that the employees were all going to get a cash bonus.

This was something that had not occurred for a number of years and represented a reward for what had been a very difficult period of turnaround for the business.

The CEO got up at the start of the event and his opening line was *"I have good news. This year there will be no redundancies!"*

This was a line he had put in his speech because he thought it was funny because it was so far removed from what he was going to announce.

Unfortunately it put into people's heads the idea of redundancy. Some of my interviewees told me that the bonus was nice but they couldn't really concentrate during the day because they had thought that the business had got past the days of redundancies.

They felt insecure about their jobs and spent most of the day thinking about how would they cope? What would they do? How were they going to look after their families?

At the lunch break they sat with others who had the same concerns and the topic dominated the lunchtime conversations.

Weeks after the event I spoke to one of the interviewees, he said his boss had to take time out in the next week to reassure the team that the business was strong and their jobs were safe.

That was a situation which should have been a cause for celebration but turned out to be a situation of great concern for many employees.

All that time and money the company had spent actually sent the company backwards not forwards. Who would spend good money to do that?

Practice finding the positive way of saying things and be aware of how you communicate. The negative approach often puts an idea in somebody's head that they were not thinking about before you mentioned it.

If you have children in your life start by thinking how you communicate with them and the responses you get.

If you often say the negative version of what you mean to say then this is a habit pattern that you have been using for many years.

Just because you have become aware of it now doesn't mean that you will automatically stop.

There is a system of awareness, increased awareness and change that will help to make the positive way a more regular habit for you.

In the first instance just be aware of when you have said the negative version of what you want to say. The more aware you are and the more often you catch yourself saying these things the more conscious you are of changing the way you communicate what you want.

You will find over time that it becomes more natural for you to communicate in a more concise positive way.

Don't forget…Sorry let me start that again and say it in the positive form. Remember….awareness is great. Catching yourself doing it wrong is making progress. All of this is moving you along the road to changing this habit.

Communicating Across Continents & Cultures

Increasingly, more people I work with are doing meetings and presentations with lots of different people from different parts of the world. And often they are together in one meeting or one webinar.

This clearly causes a complication and requires good research and a good deal of flexibility for the effective communicator. I would reiterate here that the most effective communicators know their primary audience as individuals and that is what makes such a big difference in the quality and impact of their communication.

There are plenty of generalisations made about cultures but if you think about your own culture and the individuals within that culture, you will be aware of how many people think differently about so many different ideas.

For this section I will give you a series of considerations that, if you have a large and diverse audience, will help you to improve the quality of the connection you make.

These considerations are present in most if not all the countries of the world. What differs is how the different areas are thought about or executed in those countries.

The first one is around how they are motivated when it comes to **achievement**. By that I mean is the goal in life to get as high up in business as they can or to get as much material wealth as they can or is it about family and the community.

If a culture values family and time with the family then talking to them about long hours spent accumulating more money than they need may not make the connection you want.

Alongside this is the desire of people within a culture to accept or embrace **change**.

Some cultures are all about revolutionary change to keep moving forward. Others are very much about holding onto the values and rituals that they have and have had for a long time.

Then there are customs about how people **challenge**. Many countries around the world favour a more harmonious style of communication. That means they don't like confrontation or saying no. Confrontational communication will be a turn off for them.

Connected with this is how **direct** the communication style is.

Storytelling is used a lot by some people to make a point but they do it in an indirect way. Other styles can be very direct and concise and can appear abrupt to some people.

Then there is the **role of men and women** in a culture. Some cultures will have a very different view of the role of men and women in society and again the choices you make in your presentations will have an impact on whether or not you can connect with your audience.

As there are some questions about how cultures think about the different sexes there are also questions about how they deal with **hierarchy**.

It is common to encounter hierarchy in organisations that mirrors a strict military approach. Rank is everything and you do not question the instructions of someone senior to you.

Many other cultures are much more open to the idea of everybody having a voice and everybody having a right to challenge.

The **thinking styles** can also vary. Some cultures will accept ideas if they are delivered with passion and conviction alone. Others want the most detailed proof before they will be prepared to accept an idea and then there are lots of other cultures that fit in the middle.

And to cap this list off there is a whole minefield of **handshakes, body language gestures and eye contact** dos and do nots.

This topic would comfortably justify the writing of at least another book. So I'm not going to cover this here. I have added a few thoughts on body language in Chapter 12 that relate directly to presentation styles.

To summarise this section, the key to any good communication is to know as much as you can about your primary audience.

In the absence of this detail then the above section covers some areas that are worth considering that will help your communication make that connection with more of your audience.

It is really important that you ask questions to get as much information on these areas as you can. Also if you do a lot of different presentations to different nationalities, cultures and hierarchies keep your own notes.

In the reference section at the end I have noted a couple of books that are worth reading. They are good but quite general. I have found it useful to talk to people I know within the groups to find out the things that matter more to that group.

For anyone with an interest in developing better as a multi-cultural communicator there is a wealth of information in books and on the internet and of course there is the real pleasure of going to different places and immersing yourself in the cultures and learning first hand.

In summary understand that you need to make a connection and build rapport with someone before you try to sell them your product, service or idea.

Be aware of how you communicate in terms of your use of stating things in negative language and positive language.

Where you have multinational audiences do your research to understand what amendments you can make to your style to make a connection with those audiences.

Actions:

Practice making connections before you try to sell your ideas

Be aware of negative language

Practice the positive way of saying some of your regular phrases

Consider cultural differences in style when communicating over borders

Keep a log of your own learnings when working with other cultures

Chapter 7
Selling & Buying

Are you a salesperson?

No matter what your line of work is, in fact it doesn't even matter whether or not you are employed, if you want to successfully communicate with someone you are buying and selling.

Products, services, concepts, ideas, instructions are all things that you need to sell to different people or you need to encourage them to buy those thoughts from you.

In the previous chapter we talked about getting children to follow instructions. This is a sales activity. You are trying to sell them the idea that their life is going to be better or safer if they buy into your philosophy.

Persuasion is key to achieve this. Typically there are four main reasons why you would want to persuade someone.

I'll include an acronym here because I haven't used one yet and they are a useful way to remember things. My acronym is one of your five a day its 'PEAS'.

That is:

Profit

Enjoyment
Authority
Spotlight

So you are persuading people because you want to make some **profit**. You are persuading to try and make your life more pleasurable and get more **enjoyment** from it. You want to have comfort and a little bit more control of your life and you want to demonstrate to others that you are an **authority** on the subjects you talk about. Or you want to persuade so that it is you in the **spotlight**. It's you, who has their moment, however long that is, in the Sun.

Consistently Successful buying, selling and persuading comes from listening, asking questions, understanding, empathy and knowledge and experience.

The most important thing that I want to concentrate on here is listening.

To be an excellent and effective communicator listening is going to be the skill that makes the biggest difference for you.

Other People's Words

When you really listen to what people are saying they will give you valuable clues to what are their real concerns, what are the things that make a real difference for them and they will give you insight into the language that persuades and influences them.

Words are very powerful. Our words are very powerful to us.

When it comes to our everyday language we will have key words that when everything is right we will say those words.

For me, when something is just as it should be I would describe it as "fantastic". When I use that word spontaneously, anyone around me knows that I am convinced by what I have just heard, seen or felt.

We all have our own words and most of us are unaware that we have those words. If you recorded yourself during a normal day and listened back, you would hear yourself saying certain words and phrases with conviction and you would also hear yourself using other words and phrases trying to seem as convinced when you really weren't.

You would probably notice that when you were sincere the same words or phrases were used and when you were less sincere a broader vocabulary was used.

So why does any of this matter?

Our words and our language often carry with them emotional responses, gut instinct responses. If someone describes an idea to me as "fabulous" that is a word that I relate with being frothy and probably not well thought out or costed out. My first instinct is to think this is an idea that has style but no substance.

If the same person pitches their idea as being "fantastic" and can say it with the same feeling that they would say "fabulous" chances are that I will instinctively be more open and positive about their idea.

You might be sitting there thinking surely no one would respond in that way. Well let me tell you when you start being more aware of other people's words and you use them back to them, you will be constantly surprised by the subtle but significant differences you get in their responses.

Listening to key audience members and finding their words is really useful to you when trying to get their attention and getting them to really listen.

If you talk to an audience about 'customers' and they have 'clients' then it will feel to them that you are talking about something a bit more generic that they can take or leave, rather than something that specifically applies to them.

For big groups, learning their jargon will be a big help to you. When you can replace your own terms with their jargon it feels like they are getting something bespoke.

One of the easiest ways to do this is to ask questions of people in that group. Ask them about what terminology they use and it's also useful to find any terms that turn them off.

I remember one company where the term 'workshop' was associated with communicating redundancies and so was not a term to be used when telling them about a great training opportunity.

Learning the language in meetings and one to ones is a little easier to do. It requires you to listen. Listen and find opportunities to use their words to describe key things when you are relaying information to them.

In chapter 13 the subject of low risk and no risk practice covers powerful listening techniques. Of all the things I have learned and then subsequently taught, listening skills is consistently the most powerful.

Good listening skills build rapport and often will provide additional valuable information that can make a massive difference.

I'd like to talk to you about one particular listening skill that you can practice quite easily. There are lots of different techniques but the one I have chosen to talk to you about is the one that has delivered the most success for me.

The main challenge for people trying to listen is that their minds are chattering and thinking about other things all the time. If you are having a conversation with someone you will often find that not long after they have started talking you have thought of a response.

At this stage you stop listening. Instead what you are doing is waiting for the other person to shut up so that you can say what you just thought of.

So our biggest challenge in effective listening is to create a focus. It is to give ourselves a relevant job to do that will get us to switch off our internal chatter and focus on the person we are with.

This listening technique, again with practice, does this really well.

When you are in conversation your job is to listen to the person you are having the conversation with and find opportunities to repeat some of their words back to them **as a question.**

As a question?

Yes the tone of the question and the thought when you ask them is; tell me more.

For example, a manager is telling me about a holiday experience;

Manager: "We went on holiday to New York"

*Me: "**New York?**"*

*Manager: "Yes it's a place that me and my husband have wanted to go to since we saw the film **Sleepless in Seattle**".*

*Me: "**Sleepless in Seattle?**"*

Manager: "Oh yes it's one of my favourite films and at the end Tom Hanks meets Meg Ryan at the top of the Empire State Building, I just knew I had to go there".

A conversation like this can continue for some time and what will happen through the course of it is the manager will be feeling increasing comfortable with me for two major reasons.

The first is because I am focussing on her conversation, I am actually listening. I can assure you this is really quite rare. If you think about when you are 'really' listened to, you will be aware that it is not as often as you would like.

When you are with someone who is really listening to you, you will notice that this is a very comfortable situation to be in. It is easy to get lost in the conversation and even feel like it is just you and them in the room together.

The second major reason is that by repeating their words back to them you are literally speaking their language. Each of us has an unconscious comfort with our actual words being spoken around us.

This technique is particularly useful when you need information that will help you and others around you.

I used this a lot in market research because it made people feel very comfortable around me. It also made them think more about the subjects we were talking about because the questioning style seemed comfortable and non-invasive.

Because they felt they had room and time to talk they thought beyond just their surface response and as a result were able to tell me about the things that really mattered.
When I started coaching speakers this method became invaluable to me. I would have conversations with people who needed help but weren't clear as to exactly how I could help them.

A conversation might go something like this;

Speaker: "*I lack* **confidence**".

Me: "**Confidence?**"

Speaker: "*I'm* **always not interesting** *to my audience*"

Me: "**Always, not interesting?**

Speaker: "*Well no, I suppose not. It's mainly in* **product presentations**"

Me: "**Product presentations?**"

Speaker: "*Yes, well product presentations to* **Business Directors**"

Me: "**Business Directors?**"

Speaker: "*Yes, I suppose it's when I'm around them that I feel more nervous.*"

This conversation would continue until we got down to the one or two things that I really needed to solve. If I had started working with the speaker after their first answer I could have come up with lots of different ideas to help them improve their confidence. Some might have worked, some might not have worked. It would have been a bit of a scattergun approach to solving their problem.

By asking the questions using this listening technique, I am getting the speaker to challenge their own beliefs about their capability. In the short conversation the speaker has already worked out that confidence is only a problem on a few occasions, rather than with all their presentations.

If this technique is new to you, one thought you might have is; isn't the other person likely to just stop and say "You're just repeating my words".

This is the challenge that anyone using this technique needs practice to overcome. The truth is that when you are engaged in a conversation where someone is really listening to you, your focus is on the subject you are talking about.

When you are in that situation as the person being listened to, your focus stops your mind going off and trying to analyse all the other things that are going on including what techniques the other person may be using.

Your practice is about being able to develop a focus where you listen and repeat their words as questions and that you stop analysing whether or not you will be found out.

If you are 'found out' using this technique it is because you are not focussing on the person in front of you and you're not focussing on what they are saying.

The way to comfortably practice this technique is with family and friends. If while you're practicing someone says "you're just repeating my words". You can easily tell them that you want to be a better listener so you are practicing a new technique.

Family and friends will always positively encourage this activity. I can tell you from years of feedback from course attendees that partners will be thrilled to bits that you are learning to listen better. Many attendees have told me of the rewards they have got from partners as a result of being better listeners!

As a listener once you can use this technique and switch off your own critical factor whilst doing it, you will have a very powerful way to get to the heart of what you really need to solve to create success for you and your audiences.

Other People's Names

Another thing that makes a real difference for people is using their name. Names carry great force with them. *"That was great work Michael"* carries more weight than just saying *"That was great work"*. As long as the person you are talking to is called Michael of course!

If you know the names of people in your presentation find a few opportunities to use their names. If you don't know their names then try and arrive early to your presentation and mix with your audience.

You will know yourself how much better it feels when a speaker you have not met before uses your name back to you.

Lots of people tell me they are rubbish at remembering names. In most of the cases where I have helped people it has not been so much about remembering as about actually listening in the first place.

If you want to remember someone's name then when you greet them repeat their name out loud this gives you a better chance of remembering. The next thing I usually do is associate them in my head with someone I know who has that name.

If I meet 'Jennifer' then I will say "good to meet you Jennifer" and I will likely picture Jennifer Aniston, this is a memory I already have and so I'm attaching the new person I met to that memory.

As discussed previously in the memory chapter, recall is the secret to strong memory. So periodically, I will look around at the people I have met and remind myself of their names. The more I do that the better the strength of the memory.

Hopefully by now you will have realised that whatever job you do, you are a salesperson. Remember if you are communicating there is always some level of buying and selling going on. You can be a great salesperson, the methods are relatively simple, and it's the practice that makes the difference.

People's own words have power for them and help to build rapport and make it easier for them to accept you and listen to you.

People's names also make a difference to them. Learning and using their name shows a level of respect and interest from you that will make them more comfortable with you.

Actions:

Be aware of words that you spontaneously say when something is true for you

Try doing more listening when you want to persuade

Practice ways of remembering the names of new people you meet

Use those people's names to add influence to your messages

Chapter 8
The 9 Space Considerations That Creates Success

I remember coaching at a wonderful location. There was an old industrial complex that was being refurbished. The buildings themselves were spectacular, they looked like they may have been from the Victorian era, and the complex itself was near completion but the new tenants had not moved in yet.

The people who had sourced this venue had found a gem. For the attendees this was a new and interesting venue, a great place for thinking differently. I am continually amazed by how some businesses keep finding these types of venues and turning them into great event spaces. It is an art.

The catwalk stage was set up in a gloomy old shed of a building but then superbly lit to create a great feel and look to the venue.

The only flaw was that as this venue had not been completely refurbished there were very few toilets. If you are going to bring hundreds of people to an event, you are going to need a lot of toilets. I think that may be in the top 3 of the Event Managers handbook.

To make this flaw even more challenging, the only toilets were behind the catwalk stage. If you were an audience member you needed to walk through a set of curtains behind the stage where the toilets were.

The first presenter was very lucky as there was nobody who needed the toilet. The second speaker not so. 5 minutes into their presentation the first person got up moved to the curtains, shuffled them a lot and allowed some light to spill through that created a distraction for the audience.

As if by an act of mass hypnosis, attendee after attendee had the sudden urge to use the toilet. Each time they got up they created a distraction away from the speaker on stage who soldiered on against the odds. It's very questionable as to what that audience came away with in term of messages.

Where you present has a huge impact on your success. It has a great impact on how you deliver and an even greater impact on how you and your message are received by an audience.

To make the best of your communication the venue has to work as best as it can for you and your audience. Some venue challenges cannot be overcome in the time you have and other techniques in this book will help you to manage yourself and the situation you are in to improve this experience.

This chapter deals with a variety of techniques and good preparation principles that you can employ to the benefit of you and your audience. If you prepare well and if you ask the right questions, you will be amazed by how much you can change and adapt your venue to work in your favour.

It is amazing how much a speaker will tolerate about a bad venue or set up and will soldier on because that seems to be what others have done. Just because others have tolerated it doesn't mean that it can't be changed and can't be improved.

To the less confident and experienced speaker, your stage or venue is just something you have to deal with. The cluttered space, the constant interruption caused by the walk past and staring of work colleagues and the depressing room with no windows are experiences that many of you will have had either as a speaker or an audience member.

These are all things that speakers will battle against to get through their pitch or presentation but it will often be a frustrating and irritating experience. When the pitch or presentation has been completed they will air their disappointment by saying "what else was I supposed to do? That's the only room they had!"

In this section I'm going to split the presentations into two types. One is where you have time to plan and prepare and the second is what if you just have to turn up and present.

When you have time and notice for your presentation, then making time to view and plan for your venue is essential.

Let's first talk about when you have the ability to select your space.

The things you want to consider are:

The 9 Considerations of your Presentation Space

How many people am I communicating with?
What media and furniture do I need?
Where can I present from?
Where are the power points?
Where are the lights and how do they work?
Can I do anything to control the temperature?
Is there any relevant stimulus in the room?
Is there anything in the room that is counter-productive?
How does the room smell?

How many people are you communicating with?

Knowing the size of your audience will help you to know what the right size of room is to present in. There are situations where you might feel it more beneficial to have people tightly packed into a space. If you are planning to do any interactive work then more space is likely to be beneficial.

If you are going to have your audience's attention, you need to give them space where they can see what it is you are presenting and be able to hear you properly.

What media and furniture do I need?

Do you want your audience to sit down or stand up? How long will your presentation be and if it's a longer time will the chairs be comfortable enough?

Do you need a table? Do you have notes, props and equipment that you need to keep close to you whilst you are presenting?

What media are you planning to use and is it already set up in your room? If it is already set up and you are unfamiliar with how it works, then seek out the people who do know how it works.

Having had your demonstration it is always useful to find out who can you contact if there are any media problems.

Where can I present from?

When you look at your room think about where you are going to present from. Some of us are walkers. We think better when we walk and talk. If that's you then make sure your room allows space for you to comfortably move around in.

If you do not give yourself that room then you can be distracted because 'it doesn't feel quite right.'

Someone who is naturally a walker will feel distracted by having to stand still. Very often their feet will shuffle around constantly and they will do a 'presenter dance' in the limited space they have that will look quite unnatural to their audience.

If you prefer to be grounded and still when you talk, again make sure there are adequate spaces for you to stand in. Many people in this group feel much more comfortable if they always stand on a particular side of the room or to a particular side of a screen they are projecting onto.

Check that anything you need to operate your media is comfortably available in the spaces that you choose to present from.

Where are the power points?

If you need to bring your own plug-in media then check where the power points are in the room. See if you will need additional cable to reach where you want to present from and also if you will need more plug sockets.

If you are going to be trailing wires and cables through public areas, make sure you bring some high visibility tape or covers so that your audience can walk safely around without tripping over everything.

If you are presenting at someone else's office it is worth knowing if they have any PAT rules or regulations. PAT is Portable Appliance Testing. Any company with rigourous health and safety policies may well have an issue with you plugging your own equipment into their system.

If you are unaware of PAT then look it up on your search engine of choice. It is the sort of thing that can cause delays to the start of a presentation and in some cases mean you have to use someone else's equipment to present with.

Where are the lights and how do they work?

If you are using any visual media, you will want your audience to be able to see it properly. Think about what time of day you are presenting and check that your media will work on a bright day, a gloomy day or in the evening. Depending of course on when you are presenting.

See how any blinds or curtains work in case you need to darken the room. Find out where the lights are, whether they are straight on and off or whether they dim.

I have used so many different rooms and there are so many different combinations of lights that it can sometimes take 15-20 minutes to find the lighting and learn how it works.

That is not how you would want to start your own presentation, is it?

Can I do anything to control the temperature?

The 'wrong' temperature in the room is one thing that can be a major distraction to attendees. Rooms are often considered too hot or too cold. So if a room has a heating and cooling system find out how it works.

Find out where the windows can be opened and closed and how they can be opened and closed. And if they require a key to open them, make sure you have access to that key on your presentation day.

In large groups some will be too hot and some will be too cold. My only advice there is that you should focus on what your primary audience want.

Is there any relevant stimulus in the room?

Does the room have any permanent features or displays that would be useful to create moods or additions for your presentation?

Or could you bring some props with you that would help to do that job?

I have worked a lot with the Trends & Innovation team at Clarks Shoes. They are exceptionally good at theming rooms using all sorts of different materials to lift the room and create a great environment.

They use so many types of recycled and relatively low cost materials which they then turn a variety of different spaces into fantastic and inspiring work and presentation areas. The fact that they do this also speaks volumes for them in terms of their thought and creativity.

I am constantly positively surprised by the great work they do.

You and I are a lot more creative than we give ourselves credit for. Why not research lots of different materials, lighting ideas and sound ideas and you will find some extra elements that will wow your audiences.

With the right attitude and a little bit of imagination you can create an environment which demonstrates to your audience that this could be well worth their time to attend.

Is there anything in the room that is counter-productive?

Whilst a lot of good stimulus and props can be a very positive addition, some rooms come with elements that will work against you.

It amazes me how many presentation rooms are used as temporary rubbish dumps. They are filled with files, boxes, old tills, rails of clothes from seasons past and old engine and machine parts.

Any audience member walking into a room like that is already going to be scoring you down.

Another thing that I see in companies that have more than one brand is presentations being done by one brand with another brand plastered in all areas of the audience's eye line. It often has the effect of diminishing the brand you are presenting.

All of these challenges have relatively simple solutions. Be aware of them and think about how much difference you can make by dealing with the challenges.

Give yourself time to get them sorted. Often making someone aware that their old stuff is clogging a room up will make them think about moving it. It's just that no one else ever mentioned it. But if it's your presentation and it's important to you and no one clears up then you should ensure that it gets done.

How does the room smell?

I specifically mention this one because it amazes me how tolerant presenters are of this. There are plenty of rooms that smell damp or musty or smell of old decaying lunches and this again can have an effect on how your audience are thinking and feeling.

In my kit-box I always carry a room spray. Not the sort that makes everyone choke but something that is light, pleasant and masks the unpleasant smell that exists in certain rooms.

If smells and aromas are of interest to you there are no end of articles and books that will tell you about the different effects that a range of smells will have on any group of people.

When I worked for Adams some of our stores had smells of apples in some areas of the store and baby powder in the baby section. Customers said they liked them but what was more noticeable was how many people had a very pleasant experience but were unable to spontaneously mention the aromas.

Aromas like lavender are meant to be relaxing and calming, Bergamot is said to be uplifting and cedar wood is meant to help focus and concentration.

If you are interested there are plenty of relatively cheap but good room sprays that you can experiment with and come to your own conclusions.

For the more adventurous, companies like Demeter Fragrance who I mentioned in Chapter 3 offer scents that are good for creating particular moods or memories.

It's an area where I believe there is probably some mileage. I have used some of these fragrances with smaller groups and overall I have been very pleased with the results and so have most attendees.

In my experience just having a light, pleasant aroma in a room does a very good job.

Using Different Media:

Powerpoint: Powerpoint is really good when used well. It is a support to you and not the other way round. In the most effective presentations you can use it with charts and illustrations to explain concepts that are difficult to verbalise and will use imagery to give people visual anchor points to remember important information. These charts and images can also be used as prompts for you.

For Mac users Keynote is also a really good presentation aide. This allows you to do some very impressive things with your slides. Be careful that you avoid making your presentation all about style and less about substance.

Whichever computer presentation system you use you have to be clear about the difference between a presentation pack that you would use to accompany a speaker and a handout pack.

A handout pack of slides would be used to give to someone so that they could read your presentation in your absence.

This is a very common mistake made by people using Powerpoint. A handout pack is a really good thing particularly for someone who will go to other meetings or presentations before they sit down to consider what it is they will do with your communication.

In your handout pack you may add any of your speaker notes into the slides so that any additional detail that is not on the slide is still available for the speaker.

I would recommend that you keep handout packs to the end of the presentation. This is because the moment you hand out a pack to a group of people you have lost control of their focus.

You might want to talk about the content on page 2 whilst lots of them are looking at the contents of pages 8, 9 and 10. Think about what you do when someone hands you a pack. You are a saint if you follow the pack as the speaker wants to you because most people flick through to the bits they are most interested in.

The unfortunate thing with lots of Powerpoint slides is that lots of text and bullet points are often for the speaker not the audience:

Powerpoint is a Support

- The moment this slide has gone up I have given you a challenge.
- I'm talking but you're torn between listening to me and reading this.
- If this slide was notes that I wanted to talk you through you could read it much quicker than I can read it to you.

The other problem with text slides like the one above is that because your audience can read faster than you can read to them, then they will already have made their mind up about what your slide means.

The problem for you is once they have finished reading they are not really listening to you and so if you explain something that is different to how they have read it they are just not with you. In the end they leave your presentation with a different message.

If you feel that you need to have slides like this because you have not had time to learn it or the content then help yourself and your audience out. Do this by building the bullets so that you at least keep them with you and they cannot read ahead.

The second thing to do is to keep a strict number of bullets per page. If you keep it at 3 or 4 a page then you will always know when you have finished that particular page. If a topic needs more than 4 bullets then put it over a number of pages.

If you are using two pages for a heading in your presentation then to remind yourself put in the heading "(1 of 2)" and then in the next slide put "(2 of 2)". So if you are unfamiliar with the structure of your presentation, you can at least give your audience the confidence you might know your subject by not being the most surprised one in the room when your slide has another bullet you didn't know was there!

How many times have you heard a presenter talk through their slides and clearly talk as if that slides content has concluded, only for them to click again and instead of the next slide, an additional bullet arrives at the bottom of that page.

At this point you are usually looking at a surprised or slightly embarrassed speaker. That speaker has just made their job of persuasion a little bit more difficult.

When a presentation is important to you make a presentation pack and a hand-out pack that can be given out as an aide-memoire after your presentation.

It requires extra work but if the presentation has real value to you then it is worth the effort.

Flipcharts:

Flipcharts are a great way to add energy to your presentation. If you are good at drawing, a live drawing or diagram of your subject will impress and add more credibility for you.

If you are using it for complicated numbers then pencilling the detail onto the flipchart is a way to wow your audience. This also gives you credibility with regards to the confidence in your numbers.

You lightly pencil the numbers onto the flipchart paper so that they are clear to you close up. However when you step a few feet away the numbers are not visible.

When it comes to your actual presentation you then breakaway from your Powerpoint presentation and go to the flipchart.

Here you might be telling an audience how much your idea could be worth to them.

So you talk them through by picking some numbers 'apparently' from thin air. To really impress them make the numbers difficult numbers that would not be easy to mentally multiply.

For example (and this might be what you would say):

"We know that on average we make a profit of **£87** from each unit we sold. Let's say we were comfortably able to make an extra 25% per unit using my idea that would make the profit per unit **£108**…………..and **75p** let's round that up to **£109**.

The idea would also increase unit sales. We currently sell **200,000** units. So let's say we increase that by a modest 10% that would be **220,000** units.

So previously we were making a profit of **200,000** x **£87** which is .... **£17.4 million.**

With my idea we are now selling **220,000** units at a profit of **£109** which makes............. **£23 million 980 thousand.**

Which is an additional **£6 million 580 thousand pounds!**"

The figures in bold would be written in light pencil on the board as you run your audience through your thinking process.

The benefits of this are that your credibility is greatly increased because you can add these complicated figures up right before the eyes of your audience. And because your credibility is increased, so too is the credibility of your idea.

A flipchart is also a good way to get involvement from your audience. Get them to throw numbers, words or ideas at you whilst you have another member of the audience up writing on the board. This keeps your focus firmly with the audience rather than them just seeing your back.

If they are throwing numbers at you that need calculating, involve another audience member by having them on standby with a calculator to shout out any answers.

This allows you to involve the audience and gives them a break from just listening.

Video:

A good video that supports your subject is a good tool to use.

Try to use videos that are less well known. If a YouTube video has less than 250k views worldwide you have a good chance that it will be new to most audiences. If it's above that you are lowering the chance you are showing something new.

Check how many versions of your video are on the net. Sometimes a video that seems to have a small number of views has actually been posted a number of different times and the aggregate of those views is in the millions.

When using a link to YouTube (other video sites are available!) make sure that your Wi-Fi connection will work. Despite the fantastic improvement in Wi-Fi there are still plenty of public and corporate venues that struggle due to the number of people using that network at any one time.

Ideally have the video on your hard drive so that you are not reliant on Wi-Fi connections.

Doing your own video gives you the chance of introducing something new but be careful that the quality of your videos matches the quality message you want to get across.

Software like i-movie, Sony Vegas and Avid are relatively easy to use and can produce good results. In my experience these homemade videos can work well for many presentations.

When they don't work it is often down to poor lighting when filming which creates a poor end product.

If you have a little bit of money there are a whole host of excellent freelance cameramen and editors who produce great work. A number of the freelance cameramen I've worked with I would describe as filmmakers rather than cameramen.

If you are looking for someone there are some good groups that can be located on Linkedin.com and their connections give you a selection of people you can contact to get references.

Always make sure you use a video because it supports the key points you are making. Very often a presenter will shoe-horn in a video to a presentation because the video is funny or good and because the presentation is not so good. Even though the video has nothing to do with the key messages.

Props:

Props can be good to use particularly where you want to get people involved in your presentation. Involvement in a presentation often increases understanding and the strength of your message.

In a number of my training events I use several props in different ways. I like using card magic because most people will like a card trick and its then about integrating the trick with an important element of learning.

There are other toys and props that I use which are 'outstanding' moments which make the learning more memorable. For those of you who have read the chapter about memory that will be clear to you.

Giving someone a physical prop connected to a key element of learning creates an outstanding moment in your presentation which increases the chances of them remembering that information.

I keep a collection of props some are simple things I buy some are things that I have held onto. I use an old Nokia mobile phone to show people how life has moved on rapidly in a short time. But when we talk about battery life I can talk about not all progress being great progress.

I saw a great presentation from Paul Scheele about the way the brain works when learning. It was highly interactive involving a number of audience members and a large number of toy and clothing props. I find that presentation easy to remember because of all those props and the physical activity. It works so much better than someone talking over a number of slides.

If you have read the memory chapter and the reference to 'outstanding' means nothing to you then I suggest you re-read the memory chapter 4 because somewhere you have missed the key messages.

Priming

All the attention to room, media, props and smell is about priming your audience. When you set your room up to maximum advantage you will create a lot of psychological shortcuts that will enhance the impact of your communication.

When you prepare your room well your audience will subtly pick up on the attention to detail and this can then lead them to be confident that your ideas and arguments in your presentation have been delivered in the same way.

And that's advantage to you.

But what if you have to just turn up and present in the room where everyone is already there?

This is quite a common occurrence. There are a number of things to do that will help you. The first thing is to take your time setting up. If you know it will take ten minutes to set up then tell the people who are there it will take ten minutes.

Often it's a good time to suggest a natural break and take the pressure of you as you set up.

If you are doing a presentation on your windows laptop then it's probably best to already have your laptop switched on and booted up before you go in. It can take what seems like an eternity for a windows laptop to be ready.

If you use a MacBook then make sure you have the right connector to connect it to a screen or projector.

If you have your presentation on a memory stick, check the memory stick to see what else is on there. Make your file available as soon as the contents are visible on the screen. It is better to file any other documents away into folders that are not visible.

The reason for this is because the names and content of other files can create first impressions. If your memory stick files come up and there are pictures of partners in swimwear for instance then it might not help how you are perceived.

I have lost count of the number of times someone secretively puts a memory stick into a laptop unaware that on the big screen behind them the contents are there for all to read.

The other thing I would be quick to suggest before you start is to find a comfortable space for you to present from. You will want to do the best job you can and having a space that allows you a little bit of freedom to present will help.

There is more about how to get yourself in the right frame of mind in chapter 11.

When you get it right!

Sharon Kennett is a client of mine who works for a successful agriculture company called Frontier.

Every two to three years Frontier has a staff event to inform, inspire and direct their employees. The reason why I think they do it so well is because this event is genuinely planned, prepared and practiced for the benefit of the audiences attending.

So what do Sharon and Frontier do so well?

Firstly, the event is planned months in advance. The speakers are selected and their topics are selected so that the whole day delivers chapters of the same story.

There is a dress rehearsal 3 or 4 weeks ahead of the event. Here the whole team get to hear everyone else's messages and see how their presentation fits into the day.

Any challenges they might have with delivery are identified well ahead of the event and solutions can be found for all problems (most other companies do this the day before their event).

Any significant content changes are made and this gives the speakers good time to practice with those alterations.

This dress rehearsal is done so that the range and quality of communication is improved for the benefit of the audience.

Secondly, it is the thought given to the experience of the audience. Sessions are planned with breaks so that the event is not about how much they can cram in but instead it's about improving the audience's ability to remember key ideas.

All members of staff are invited and the event is repeated over 3 or 4 days so that the business can continue to run effectively for their customers and the invitees can relax knowing that someone else is covering them for the day.

Employees with disabilities are informed before the event of the arrangements that have been made for them at the event so that they can avoid unnecessary worry.

At the last event I had the good fortune to sit at a table with some of the employees. This gave me the chance to make notes for the speakers and also to see how the event was being received by the employees.

At the table I was at there was some water, cordial and a bowl of mint imperials. After the first session the audience went off for their coffee break. When they came back some nice chocolates had been added to the table.

I was positively surprised by how good an impact this addition had made. People were genuinely delighted by the addition of chocolates.

Having worked with Frontier for a few years this should not have been a surprise. Any company that really understands the value of communication would consider an event down to the level of making the changes to the table sweets.

In all my years of working at conference events I have never seen feedback results from a conference as consistently good as those from Frontier.

Their employees appreciate the events because from start to finish the event is done for the benefit of the employees.

The work that the Senior Leadership Team put in is significant and as an employee of the company that hard work comes through. It reminds the audience that they have made a good choice to work for Frontier and it also tells them they are in very good hands.

This type of investment in communication is rarer than it should be.

To summarise, you can make a big impact to the effectiveness of your communication if you put some time and effort into thinking about where and how you are going to present and what impact that will have on your audience.

Actions:

When preparing your venue think about the 9 considerations of your presentation space

Use Powerpoint as a support to you, do not let Powerpoint lead your presentation

Consider creating a Presentation Pack and a Hand-Out pack for important presentations

Use flipcharts for a change of media

Use pre-created flipcharts to create impact

Use video where it can support your ideas, not just because it's a good video

Collect props that can be used to illustrate keypoints and create a different dynamic and audience involvement

Chapter 9
A Digression…....

In 1985 I joined Adams Childrenswear as a stock controller. I joined in November and from November through to the following July there was a general pattern to the day.

We started work at 8.50am there was a reasonably full morning processing and chasing deliveries, taking calls, having a coffee break, liaising with colleagues from other departments and attending the occasional meeting. Then there was lunch at 12.30 for 45 minutes and then an afternoon similar to the morning.

If no one rang late in the afternoon, then myself and my colleagues would sit from about 4.45pm with empty work trays, waiting for 5pm so we could officially stop work and go home.

This was a time when clothing stores in the UK ran their ranges across two seasons. There was spring/summer and there was autumn/winter. There was no overlap. Spring/summer clothes arrived in the shops in February at the end of the January sales. And autumn/winter arrived in August at the end of the July summer sale.

I didn't realise at the time that work would never be like that again. The next season the business continued to grow its number of shops, increased the size of the ranges and started to stock ranges that overlapped seasons. All of this extra activity increased the phonecalls and workload.

From then on I always left work at night, with jobs that still needed to be done. I can't remember another time in that job when my in-trays were empty!

These days I always have work that needs doing tomorrow. There is no longer enough time in the day to get all my work done. Everyone I meet talks about the same thing. There are always plans, projects, accounts, calls, emails, reports and a variety of other things that will need doing.

It is a case of getting the things done that need to be done the quickest. Sometimes that is the thing of most value and other times it can be the thing that stops somebody chasing me up constantly.

When I was working full time for a business there was always some motivator to get this work done. There was someone else who would chase me for it. Managers, Directors and Supervisors were there to remind me of which job carried the most importance at that time. There was always something that would fall down if I didn't do it and there was always the potential that I would put my job at risk if I missed work deadlines.

All of these things can give most people the motivation they need to get work done.

When you work for yourself it can be different. If it's work that a client expects and needs doing for you to get paid, that can be a motivator. If it's something that is vital to them or their business then they will phone, text or email you so that you are very aware that it needs doing and needs doing soon.

But what about a new course to design? What about a great presentation that you could do but no one has asked you to do yet? And what about that bit of accounting work that needs to be prepared before everything is handed to your accountant? What about that book that you said you always wanted to write?

Not only that, but for me this type of work is done at my office at home. The distractions are all there for me: TV sport, TV box sets, TED talks, tea, biscuits, phoning friends, checking email, social media and interesting websites, games of FreeCell and Angry Birds. So many distractions.

The distractions are endless and they always appear more attractive when there is other work to do. The challenge is that the sort of work I need to do when working at home is the work I find the hardest to get to grips with. I love delivering presentations and training courses but putting them together lacks excitement for me. There are times when I can work on my own but there are other times when I feel much more comfortable and inspired when there is the noise of other people around me.

I do love it when sessions come together and it's great fun for me to practice them, but coming up with ideas from cold without a specific use for them at that moment in time, well, that's difficult. I am more motivated to move away from something that is painful rather than to chase after something that will add to what I already have.

The technique that works for me is to organise a to-do list the night before, prioritise the activities and then put together rewards for achieving each of the items on the to-do list. So, no cup of tea until I have completed the first major task of the day. Anyone who knows me knows I love my tea.

Some people reward themselves with food treats, making a social phone call, a bit of Facebook time, even allowing themselves to check their own email and I'm sure you have your own version of a reward.

Back in the summer of 2008 I was pulling together a Storytelling course. I was doing this whilst the Beijing Olympics was in full flow. I'm one of those people who doesn't watch athletics very often but if you put it into an Olympic Games then suddenly I'm very interested.

For me this was ideal. Every day was full of races or events that I would like to watch. I would have a look at the order of events the night before and identify which races or activities I really wanted to see.

There is something about watching these races live that adds a great deal of tension and enjoyment to it. Somehow watching a recorded version of the race doesn't carry with it the same level of tension or enjoyment and there is a possibility you will find out the result before you actually get to sit down and watch it.

So, there were my rewards, if I did the work on time I could pop down to the lounge put the TV on and watch the 100m sprint or a swimming event. And very often do it having also earned myself a cup of tea and a biscuit.

If not then I had set the events to be recorded at the start of the day and I could go and watch those events only when I had completed the work related to that reward.

One day I had chosen to watch the 400m women's final. I completed the action of the part of the course that was related to finding your own stories and completed it 20 minutes before the start of the race. That meant a cup of tea and I could also listen to the pre-race build up. For those of you that watched events for the 2012 Olympics you will be aware that some of the pre-race commentary gives you a lot of information that can make the event even more interesting or meaningful for you.

For most of the other races, I got there just as they were starting because I under-estimated how much time it would take to get the sections finished. This meant watching the race but not necessarily understanding much about the athletes taking part, who was expected to win and who to watch out for.

In this event, the Women's 400m, Christine Ohoruogu was running for Great Britain. When there are people running from your own nation it can add something to the tension and potential enjoyment or disappointment.

The commentators were saying that if everyone ran to form then there was a chance that Christine could get a bronze medal. She was up against Sanya Richards of the United States who appeared to be most people's favourite for a gold medal.

Then there was Shericka Williams of Jamaica. She was another talented runner who had a chance of gold but most were tipping her for silver.

Then there were a talented trio of Russian athletes. Yulia Gushchina who was fancied for silver or bronze and also fancied to push for gold. And then there was Tatiana Firova and Anastacia Kapachinskaya who were a decent bet for silver or bronze.

If you can imagine what the start of a 400m race looks like, the track had nine lines and as you looked from left to right the lanes were numbered 9 down to 1. At the start the runners are in their lanes but they are some distant apart from the other runners.

This is because the person on the outside has further to run on the outside bend than the person on the inside. So the person in lane 9 is much closer to the camera as you look than the person in lane 1.

The principal athletes were placed in the following lanes. Kapachinskaya was on the outside in lane 9, Sanya Richards, the favourite, was in lane 7, Shericka Williams was in lane 6 Gushchina was in lane 5, Christine Ohoruogu was in lane 4 and Tatiana Firova was in lane 3.

The runners were ready to start, they were on their marks, the race was ready to start. And then the gun sounded and they were away. From the start Sanya Richards, knowing the main threats were behind her, set off at a blistering pace to put some distance between her and her main competitors.

Shericka Williams got into her stride and ran a comfortable first hundred metres not concerned by the fact that Richards had put a big distance between them.

But after passing the 100 metre mark Gushchina stepped up her speed worried about the gap between her and Richards and in doing so appeared to overtake Williams.

Williams was thrown by the Russian going past her on the inside and stepped up her own pace and broke the rhythm she had been running.

After 200 metres Kapachinskaya in lane 9 and Firova in lane 3 seemed to also be concerned by the distance and changed their running style to reduce that distance.

All the time this was going on, Christine Ohoruogu ran a consistent pace and did not react to all the actions and reactions of her competitors.

After 300 metres the runners are coming into the final 100 metre straight. As a casual watcher of athletics, this is the first real time when you can see for yourself where everybody is because now the person in front is clear.

Richards was way out in front and then behind her were two of the Russians, Gushchina was second and Firova was third. In fourth place was Christine.

With 50 metres to go Richards was still in front but the gap was closing. The problem for her was that she looked like she had no more to give, she was running out of energy and trying desperately to hold on. Gushchina and Firova still held second and third but they also looked spent having used their energy to close the gap.

With 20 metres to, Christine Ohoruogu started to move through into first place. A little behind her was Shericka Williams who, after the wobble of trying to respond to Gushchina passing her on the inside, had gone back to running at her own pace.

Ohoruogu and Williams moved comfortably through into first and second place looking quite comfortable whilst the two Russians and the American looked in great pain but seemed unable to find any extra energy to respond.

Christine Ohoruogu crossed the line winning the gold medal, Shericka Williams got the silver and Sanya Richards had to settle for bronze.

It was a thrilling race to watch and all finished in less than 50 seconds.

Watching that race I took a huge lesson from it. Christine Ohoruogu won that race because she set out to run the best 400 metres that she could. If she ran her best 400 metres then she couldn't ask for much more.

All of the other competitors ran all or part of their race as a response to what was happening around them. The game plans of their competitors made them change what they were going to do. None of the others ran their best 400 metres and as a result of that it was Christine, not them, who won gold.

How many times in your life have you stopped yourself from being your best because you are responding to what other people are doing around you?

Chapter 10
……Into Storytelling

I am very grateful to a master hypnotist called Igor Ledochowski, who has taught me the value and power of storytelling.

I have attended a number of his courses and he is a brilliant exponent of storytelling to teach and engage.

The story in the previous chapter is one I told to a group of area & regional managers at the start of a training session.

I had been given the after lunch slot. I don't believe any time slot is more difficult than any other. But I do believe that different considerations need to be thought of when addressing audiences at different times of the day.

I walked through the group whilst they were having their buffet lunch on my way to set up in the presentation room.

Many of them seemed happy, chatting away with their colleagues but at various corners of the room and outside the room there were various executives on their phones. Most we're looking troubled.

They had been out of contact throughout the morning and as most area & regional managers will know, most of the calls they receive in this situation are likely to be challenges or bad news.

Looking at some of the faces, I started to question the session I had planned to open the training with. Some of those people would be physically present but their minds would be outside thinking about what they had just heard on their phones and they would be trying to solve various problems of which they were now aware.

Instead, I sat down and wrote a framework for a story that I would use to open the session. My objective for that part of the presentation was to get them focussed back into the activities they were going to do in the afternoon. And it was also to get them into a positive headspace that would make them much more prepared to engage and get involved in the sessions.

So now I will deconstruct the story that I told you in the previous chapter.

Lunchtime was now over. The attendees came into the room. It was an excellent room with tiered seating and a neat and compact stage at the front. As they settled down I looked around at the faces and as I expected I could see some of them were lost deep in their own thoughts.

Without saying anything else I started telling my story and **stage one** was to **introduce confusion**.

Most of them would have expected some kind of introduction, possibly an agenda of what we might be doing.

At the very least they might have expected a "hello" or "good afternoon". Instead I appeared to be chatting about trivia.

As I chatted, the more trivial the better, I looked around the room and could see those distracted people were paying attention to me and that most of them were looking confused. Confusion is good at times because it tends to bring focus.

People have to pay conscious attention in order to work out what is happening. This focus tends to mean having to let go of the other things they were thinking about and bring their attention firmly into now.

Stage 2 involved making a connection and building some rapport. The story continued to talk about things I experienced that I know to be common.

Always having too much work to do, rewarding myself for tasks done, being distracted by email, these are relatively common experiences that this audience could relate to.

As I told this part of the story I looked around at the audiences, I was looking to see that I was getting a lot of nodding heads agreeing with different parts of the presentation.

I refer to this stage as the start of **funnelling**.

For me this is about throwing out a range of non-specific ideas where people are able to bring their own experiences to them. For example;

I could say to you "You know when you are packing your bags for a holiday to Las Vegas."

I might be connecting with a number of you but I might lose a lot of you when I specifically reference Las Vegas. If that is not a place where you have been. Instead I would say;

"You know when you are packing your bags for that holiday or vacation."

This does the job of being more general and also adds the word vacation for those people that don't use the word holiday.

Quite rightly you will point out that there are many people who have managed to get through life without having to pack their own bags.

That's why you throw out a range of general statements. And it's also why you pay close attention to your audience to see their reaction. As soon as you have got heads nodding and good eye-contact, you know it's time to move on.

If you relook at the story in the previous chapter you will see a variety of statements that have little to do with the story but instead are designed to make a connection with people. I am looking for them to have the sort of response that says "Yes, I do that" or "Yes, I think that".

Back to the story. Once I had got the attention of the entire group and had had all of them nodding their head at some point, I moved on to stage 3.

Stage 3 is the continuation of funnelling. This is where having got their attention you now focus them into an area where you can get your key message across.

This is where the funnel begins to narrow.

In this instance my goal was to get them into the right positive and attentive state to get the most out of the training session.

At this stage the funnel is narrowing in as you add references that are much more specific and are leading the audience to where you want them to be.

This works because when you create rapport with your audience in Stage 2 they are engaged and connected and they will happily follow the flow of your story.

In all elements of the storytelling it is much more effective if you really engage in your story. A good story is often told physically as well as verbally.

What I mean by that is when I was talking about the lanes the runners were in, I was using my hands to map out the relative positions of the runners at the start. I paced the telling of the story with the stages of the race. As I talked through each 100 metres, the pace of the story got quicker and quicker.

One of the really important things that Igor taught me is that if you want people to occupy a particular mood or headspace then go there yourself first and then encourage the people to follow you.

A great story is the storyteller experiencing the story as they tell it and that is what makes it so compelling for the audience that is listening intently.

The Christine Ohoruogu story is my take on the experience of that race. I saw people choosing to run a race to negate a threat at the expense of running their best race. And I watched Christine set out to run her best 400m regardless of what others were doing and I had seen her win that race.

The moral of succeeding through being your best and not being distracted by your competition was a moral that reflected the success of the business I was working with and also demonstrated that on that day I wanted them to gauge their progress by their own standards and not those of the other people around them.

You will be pleased to know that the session was very successful and very enjoyable to do.

Training good, open people is one of the things that makes my job so enjoyable. If you have attended any of my training thank you, I hope I have made the positive impact on you that you have made on me.

Back to the story again. The great thing about that story is that before I wrote this book, I have never actually written that story down. The beauty of stories and storytelling is that it does not matter what age you are or from where in the world you come from, a lot of information that you possess has been passed to you by stories.

To summarise Funnelling in Storytelling;

Storytelling is a great way to start a presentation and to get people into the right state for your presentation.

In storytelling you should look for connections to make with people. Use common experiences such as the chore of getting to work, frustration of hanging on for call centres, a holiday experience, working longer hours or working at home and there are many, many others. Look at your audience as you tell your story and you can tell from their attention, or lack of it, if you are making a connection.

If you are unsure of common connectors pick up any newspaper and have a look at the horoscopes. They are full of general phrases and connections to the point that you could read all twelve horoscopes to someone and they could probably say yes to around 70% of what they have heard.

Whilst some of you will be thinking horoscopes are a load of rubbish you will be aware that there are a huge number of people who think there might be something to them.

That is the power of making connections through funnelling. If you make enough random statements, the sheer volume of correct statements that land with your audience gives them the sense that you are specifically talking about them and to them.

Then, once you have that connection, you tell the part of your story that will take them to the appropriate state for your presentation. It might be a story of perseverance, a story of adversity, a story of innovation or a story of trust. Good stories are available everywhere, the internet, books, other peoples presentations.

This method is like a funnel where at the broad end you are talking about general common matters that make connections but the more you tell a story the more you funnel people to the main idea or purpose of your communication.

Because you have connected with them first, most will follow your flow and listen better as a result.

When you find good stories you like make a note of them. When you tell them indulge yourself and paint pictures in your audiences mind, this will get their attention and get them open to what they are going to hear next.

The most important thing with any stories you choose is that they engage you. If you have a story that you think is only 'alright' it is unlikely that you will be able to connect with it in a way that will make it compelling and engaging for your audience.

Find stories that move and inspire you. Think about how those stories relate to you and also add your own spin on that story.

A good story can be told by many different people and by adding their different take on the story it means each telling of that story brings a different experience and meaning to a single audience.

That story is an example of a **teaching story**. In a teaching story you can give an example with a moral or a teaching point and in telling the story prove your point to those that listen.

Teaching stories can be about people and things that your audience know a little about or it can be about something or someone that they know nothing about.

I particularly like stories that tell me something new that I was unaware of or that give me extra details about a story that I thought I knew.

These stories can be from your own experience or from other people's experiences.

In the earlier chapter 5 about opening and closing I said there was a much better way to introduce yourself and that is a **Who am I** story.

In a who am I story instead of just saying your name and a CV you can take an element of your life and career to date and tell a story that informs your audience of who you really are.

That could be a story about your personal values, the way that people work with you and for you, it could be a story of what was it that got you to do the job that you are doing now.

This is much more powerful because you can use the elements of storytelling to make connections and build rapport. In your story you are not just saying I did this job or that job, instead you are telling them how you did and why you did it. Information that often better informs an audience of who you are and how you work and more importantly why they should listen to you.

When this is done well it is fantastic. One word of caution though. This type of story is most effective when the story you tell is related to the objectives you have for your presentation.

Avoid adding this onto every presentation if it has no connection to your principal objectives.

One other type of story that I find particularly useful is an **empathy** story. In an empathy story you can demonstrate to an audience that you understand how they might be thinking and feeling about the topic you are going to talk about.

In a way you are telling them that you know what they are thinking about.

In acknowledging your similar experience you can keep their critical factor open because you are talking as someone with a relatable experience. This is particularly effective if you can tell in your story how you came through this and offer them lots of hope. This is hope that there is a solution and hope that you are the person who can guide them through this.

To summarise; I have only mentioned a couple of types of stories. I teach courses just on the subject of storytelling because there is so much in it. I would guarantee you that most of the really compelling presentations that you have listened to have included storytelling.

There are plenty of other story types that I have not mentioned. The important thing is not to know all the types of stories in a theoretical way, instead it is about having your own range of stories and practicing your stories in different situations.

You will find that all the elements you need to present on can be improved by including a storytelling element.

I would say that the consistently best, most effective and most enjoyable presentations follow a story format. They are powerful to listen to, much more easily retold and they are very enjoyable to deliver.

Actions:

Find opportunities for bringing storytelling into your presentation

Practice funnelling when talking with groups of people

Pay attention to when you have got the attention of people in groups

Think of stories in your life that you can attach teaching lessons to

Chapter 11
Take Control of the One Person You Can Manage

I spent a lot of years in the process of being managed by managers or managing other people. I learned a little bit more from each experience but on the whole I just got on with it and hoped my experience would get me through.

Then one day I was listening to a Peter Thomson interview and he talked about managing other people being a myth.

You cannot really manage people. Instead you manage the one person you can manage and that's you. You can manage how you respond to people, situations and pressure in order to try and get the outcomes you need.

The great thing about this is that you will already have lots of experience whether it has been in work, with family or in social situations where you have persuaded, inspired or directed someone else to do something to help make your life, and hopefully, their life better.

And you have done this because you have been managing how you have responded to them and the situation you were in.

When you think about it you may also become aware of the way you have spoken to these people when you wanted to help them. You listen properly, you let them talk. If they are unnecessarily harsh on themselves you would pick them up on it.
Yet sometimes the way we talk to ourselves is brutal and actually unhelpful. We are sometimes unaware of what we are saying when we talk to ourselves and the impact it has.

How often have you knocked over a cup or mug and broken it and then heard yourself say "you're stupid." In that situation you are giving yourself a permanent statement (you're stupid) for an individual event. You do not spend every minute of everyday breaking crockery so the label you have given yourself is too strong.

The reason why this matters is because this self-talk has a big impact on your physical response to people and situations.

There are lots of people who tell themselves they can't do this or they can't do that to the point that they believe it and it becomes a self-fulfilling prophecy.

In my career I have encountered lots of people who have said that they cannot do presentations, that they are incapable of being a public speaker.

As long as that person wants to be good at public speaking then they can always be helped and made to be a good presenter.

The challenging people who don't make it are those who genuinely have no desire to do it. No interest, no practice, no success.

You have picked this book up because you want to be the best speaker and presenter you can be. So the next thing you and I need to work on is your self-talk.

At this stage if you are saying to yourself "I am no good at public speaking", then minimise how that feels by saying "I'm not as good as I want to be......now"
And then add "But I know I can be with good practice."

The first statement is a permanent statement. "I am no good". The second statement is a situational statement. It is an honest statement and so it will feel true for you. And it also references that the situation can change positively for you if you take the right action.

Say both of those things again and notice how different you feel when you say the second statement and how much more in control and how much more capable you feel with the second statement.

"I am no good at public speaking"

"I'm not as good as I want to be, now. But I know I can be with good practice".

Keep saying these two things until you genuinely feel the positive difference that you get from saying the second statement.

Make anything that you are disappointed about with yourself situational and not permanent and it will make you feel stronger and more capable to progress.

Confidence:

Some coaching sessions can be a little bit like walking along the Yellow Brick Road from Wizard of Oz because inevitably somebody will want more courage and confidence.

For those of you that are not familiar with the Wizard of Oz, the films heroine is Dorothy a young girl who just wants to get back home. On her journey she meets a scarecrow that wants a brain, a tinman who wants a heart and a cowardly lion who is looking for courage. They go to see the Wizard in the hope he can give them these things.

It turns out that they always had the ability to get those things for themselves.

Confidence is increased by marginal gains in all areas of your preparation. If you have prepared your objectives well, know enough about your audience, prepared your presentation and your media, used memory techniques to learn your key points and planned and set up your room it is amazing how much confidence this will bring you.

Some people in this situation say to me "Yes but I still have butterflies." The next time you are positively excited about something notice where you feel that. It often manifests itself as butterflies in the stomach.

Too many speakers misread butterflies as fear when they are more usually a combination of a little fear and a lot of excitement.

The excitement comes from the idea of standing up in front of a group and doing something so well that it engages and inspires an audience.

For me I would rather have butterflies because it is a sign to me that what I am about to do matters. The feeling can be managed by a number of techniques.

The most effective one for me is focus. When it is my time to stand up and talk I think about how should I be at the opening of my presentation. Do I want to look concerned? Do I want to look happy? What should I be thinking about that will help me to deliver my first line.

When you consciously focus on your job, when you focus on managing yourself, the effects of butterflies tends to diminish dramatically.

For an extra boost there is a technique that works surprisingly well. First find somewhere you can do this where you won't be disturbed. It is a technique I read about and then later on I saw a TEDtalk by Amy Cuddy that added the scientific evidence for doing this.

For 2 minutes make your body as big as you can by adopting your Superman or Wonder Woman pose.

Make sure that as many of your body parts as possible are extended out trying to make yourself as big as possible. Puff your chest out, have your elbows out as wide as they can go and have your head held up so that you are looking straight ahead without putting any strain on your neck.

Do this while you have your feet flat on the floor just a little more than shoulder width apart, so that your body is strong and stable.

Scientific studies have shown that doing this increases testosterone, which increases confidence, and reduces cortisol, that is a contributor to stress.

Either do it privately where you won't feel self-conscious or convince the people around you to join in, most of them will thank you for how they feel or at least have a laugh with everybody doing their best Superman or Wonder Woman.

There are lots of other techniques such as anchoring, an Neuro Linguistic Programming (NLP) exercise that helps you connect quickly with useful feelings such as confidence, resolve and happiness.

If you want to know about these things they will be covered on most good one day NLP courses. They are good and useful techniques but I see them as a plaster when someone needs help.

I would much rather you knew the benefits to managing you that you will get from good organisation, preparation and practice. If you want to be a truly great presenter that attitude will get you significantly further.

In summary you can't really manage other people you can only manage yourself and how you respond. The way you talk to yourself is important. If something isn't working for you then describe it to yourself in a situational way, such as it's not working for me now.

Confidence comes most from good preparation and practice. The better you prepare and practice the more you believe in your own presentation. If you want a short-term confidence boost adopting a Superman or Wonderwoman pose will give you that.

Actions:

Be aware of how you talk to yourself

Learn to talk to yourself as if you are someone you wanted to help

Talk about challenges to yourself as a situational problem not a permanent problem

Use the steps in this book to prepare well

As you add each element of good preparation, be aware of how your confidence and your excitement grows

Practice your Superman and Wonder Woman pose

For other quick fix confidence boosts look at NLP books and courses

Chapter 12
A few Thoughts About Body Language

One of my favourite words is verisimilitude. It means 'the appearance of truth.' In presenting this means those moments when your words, your tone and your body language all match to demonstrate to your audience that what you are saying is something that you totally believe in.

To be the most authentic, effective speaker that you can be you always need to be true to who you are. The person that your audience meets and talks to when you are off the stage cannot be someone completely different to the person they have just listened to.

In this chapter we are going to cover some elements about body language. We are going to talk about the things that most often come up as questions from the people I have worked with over the last 15 years.

Lots of people that I work with ask the question "what do I do with my hands?" This is often asked as a result of other people saying 'your hands move about a lot when you talk.' The problem is this is perceived as a bad thing.

If someone offers you this advice consider the following. Are they interested in the subject you are talking about? Very often when people offer this feedback it's because they weren't listening to you because they are not interested in that subject and so the only thing they can comment on is how distracted they were by your hand movements.

In cases like that, if a cat walked by they would have probably have been distracted. Their feedback, although from a good place, is probably unhelpful.

If you use your hands when you talk, no matter how much or how little, they are an important part of how well you communicate.

If you are a hand talker and you try to suppress the movement of your hands you will be aware that it can also suppress your tone, your vocal variety and your enthusiasm.

Now is the time to understand that hand movements when you talk are part of you as a great and effective communicator.

If you filmed yourself talking naturally then you would notice that the hand movements happen in anticipation of what you are saying. The right movement accompanies the right words.

People who try to add hand movement for emphasis when it's not natural often have the hand movements happen slightly later than when the words are said. This leads to audiences feeling that something is not right or true.

The most common uses of this seem to have appeared and spread in British Politics over the past couple of decades. I am not sure how these politicians are practicing but they are using gestures that look like they have been consciously choreographed rather than being natural.

Trust is a huge challenge in politics and I believe that this practice of choreographed gestures is detrimental to improving the believability of politicians.

Compare any recent party conference speech from any of the major parties to most TEDtalks and you will see a huge difference in natural delivery.

In the political speeches you can almost see the mental considerations of 'I'm talking about freedom, now I need to move my hands like this.' Compare that against the natural flow of a TEDtalk with a speaker totally engaged with their subject matter and you will find that you are not distracted by their hand and arm movements.

All body language gestures can be practiced and added to your performance with the key being that they look and feel natural.

The endgame for you is for these movements to happen without you being consciously aware that they are happening.

In a presentation you should always have any moves be driven by a natural thought and be happening to you rather than because you planned to do it.

Another important part of body language is to do with how your ability to think is connected with movement or stillness.

In short; are you a stander or a walker?

Some people find that they are able to think better and remember better if they are walking as they talk. Once you recognise if this is you, you will perform better if you allow yourself presenting spaces that give you some freedom to move.

If you think better when you are stable and still, then it is good to practice standing with your feet slightly more than shoulder width apart. You want to make sure that when you think about how the pressure on each leg feels, they both feel like they have equal weight on them.

This way you can comfortably stand like this for a reasonable amount of time.

If you have more weight on one leg than the other then that will tire quicker. This will force you to switch the balance of your weight to the other leg. Because more weight is on that leg, it too will tire. So you switch back to the other leg. It hasn't had time to fully recover so you can only put weight on that for a shorter period. So you switch again.

This happens until the speed of leg adjustments create some kind of strange 'presenter dance' that will be a distraction for the audience.

Be aware of physical comfort when you are presenting because if you get physical comfort right it will often help to increase your psychological comfort.

Talking of psychological comfort, to manage yourself when you are talking to a group you need to be as relaxed as you can be. It will help you to think better and will make your memory easier to access.

The key element I am talking about here is about removing tension from your body. If when you talk you are aware of your hands being gripped together or held tightly behind your back then you need to just let go and relax.

When you are talking to groups there are all sorts of messages being sent from your brain to your body. Tension in your body will usually send messages to your brain that something is wrong. The problem when you are speaking is that you are trying to remember lots of things, you are focussing on the audience, thinking about what is coming next and then what is coming after that.

Any other tension signals that arrive in your brain saying 'something is wrong' can be misinterpreted by you in this situation. You may feel that the presentation is going wrong.

When you are talking in presentations and meetings be aware of how you are sitting or standing. Are your hands clasped into fists? Are you gripping your own wrists or arms unnecessarily tightly?

If you find yourself doing this then just relax the grip. The more often you do it the more practiced you will be at doing this in moments of high tension and the better and more in control you will feel when you relax.

There is a theory that when you are tense the more instinctive parts of your brain take control and it is harder for your whole brain to connect and communicate in the way you would like.

This results in you finding it difficult to recall information that you know you know really well. The moment you are relaxed that information freely flows to you.

Relaxation and control are important tools for you to be a great presenter. It's important that you understand the connection between how you stand and hold your body and the positive or negative impact it has on how well you think and feel.

Practicing some techniques with body language can be very useful for you. I say this with the caveat that you practice so often that it becomes natural and normal and not choreographed like some of our politicians.

The Human Timeline:

When you are in front of an audience consider yourself on a graph. If you are talking about the past stand on the left hand side (as your audience sees it).

And when you talk about the present or future move to the right as the audience see it.

Each time you talk about the past, present or future if you stand in the right place you will have established a psychological timeline in your audiences mind.

You can then use this to your advantage by talking about a problem that no longer exists and standing in the past area, they will find this more believable if you have established your timeline.

And then you can talk about a positive outcome in the present or future. Again making it seem more credible to your audience.

This works because psychologically everything that has been said in one area refers to the past and everything said in the other area refers to the future.

Years of training and immersion has taught us to see charts display the past on the left hand side as we look and the future going to the right. This psychological shorthand makes it easy for our brain to adopt this same logic when we are looking at a presenter who is subtly mapping that graph out for us.

Practice the idea of using the directions that makes sense to the way an audience would see it rather than the way you see it and this will increase their understanding of your messages.

It's a simple technique that works again and again.

Yes and No Spaces:

This next idea works exceptionally well with practice. For this explanation I will demonstrate how it works for right handers seeing as they outnumber both ambidextrous people and left handed people.

So if you are right handed, whenever you make a positive point, make a small gesture with your right hand held above waist level and out to the side. This creates an area in space that is associated with a positive 'Yes' response.

Anytime you say something negative make a small gesture with your left hand below waist height and down by your side. If you do this often enough you will create a "No" space.

You can then use this when you want to influence people to make a decision without appearing to favour either of the ideas, making them feel they have made a free choice. Your choice.

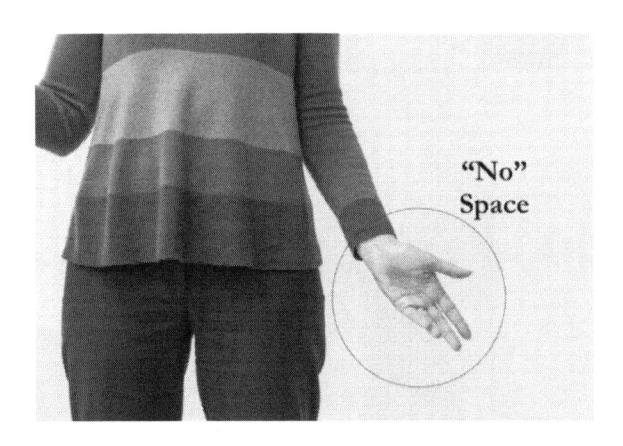

The example below is a sample illustration of how this might be employed. When using this idea these subtle moves would be happening throughout the presentation to create maximum impact.

Imagine our company has two choices the one I favour and the one someone else favours. I do not want to just rubbish the other option because that might make me look narrow minded. Instead I choose to use this method to subtly bring doubt to 'his' option for the listening audience.

For this first section each point is accompanied by a small subtle hand gesture (g1) with the left hand below waist height and down by my side;

"After the bank crash in 2007 (g1), customer confidence crashed (g1), people stopped buying (g1), companies were reluctant to invest (g1), all you heard on the news was bad news now (g1) and bad news to come (g1). For a long while it felt like things might never get better (g1)".

For this next session each point is accompanied by a small subtle hand gesture (g2) this time with the right hand above waist height and out to the side;

"In the last couple of years things have started to pick up (g2), good news started to come in (g2), slowly at first but then it has got stronger (g2) and stronger (g2). Confidence has grown significantly (g2), companies are investing again (g2) and future growth looks very good (g2).

Now that I have set a market context for the situation we are in I then present the two options apparently objectively but at the end I ask my audience a question and give them a choice;

"Do you want to choose 'his' option (g1) or 'my' option (g2)?"

The result of this for the audience is to create doubt in 'his' option without really being able to put their finger on why it feels like a less successful option.

It has worked on many occasions for me and many other people I have worked with. The great thing about this is very often during a good presenter's speech I am unaware that they are doing this because it is done so naturally.

One word of warning. All of this assumes that you are comparing two reasonable options. A psychological method like this will not compensate for a truly awful idea.

On a practical level, if you are left handed then reverse the above instructions.

The reason why you would use your dominant hand for the 'Yes' area is that intuitively it feels more right (no pun intended) when you do it and tends to be a more natural move for you. The ambidextrous among you take your pick.

This takes a lot of conscious practice before it becomes second nature. The great thing is if you practice it a lot you will find you are totally unaware that you are doing it. This has the effect of being more natural and more impactful.

Presenting As A Team:

There are some key thoughts and ideas that will benefit most team presentations.

Pay attention to your team mates when they are presenting. If you are not interested then why should an audience be interested?

Before going up as a group, try and see the space you are presenting in and decide how you will group yourself and who will stand where. To walk up to your presentation and walk straight to your places creates a very good first impression.

Often saying "I'm going to handover to Johnny" looks cheesy and can be a turnoff to audiences. Also most audiences aren't interested in you saying thank you to each other when you handover. They want to know what you have to say and how it applies to them. In most cases they want you just to get on with it.

For the most professional presentations use non-verbal signals to smoothly handover. If you are using a PowerPoint clicker, when you finish your section walk to the next speaker, hand them the clicker and let them start their section.

Again the best team presentations are practiced. They look clean, cohesive and concise. These traits make a team really look like a team.

In summary, there is a wealth of information on body language and when you allow yourself to use it well as part of your communication you will see some great results.

By all means read more about the subject and watch lots of good and bad presentations to see it in action. But I would suggest your most successful avenue is to become more aware of your own body language in all communication situations.

Watch filmed presentations of yourself, objectively, note what makes you at your most comfortable and in control and notice the times where the opposite is true.

Allow your body to do what it does and make it a positive contributor to your presentations.

Actions:

Allow your hands to be free when you talk to allow for true hand gestures

If you are happier walking, find room in your presentation area to walk

If you are more comfortable standing still practice standing with your feet slightly more than shoulder width apart to stay still longer

Practice using your presentation space as a timeline

Practice using 'yes' and 'no 'areas with your hands

Pay attention to colleagues when presenting as a team

Practice any team presentation to make you look like a team

Chapter 13
Low Risk & No Risk Practice

I hope up to now you've found some really interesting, thoughtful and useful ideas that will help you to give the best performance of you.

Knowledge is a fantastic thing but the thing that really makes the difference for you is the application of knowledge.

People will go and buy lots of fantastic books, CDs, DVDs and online courses that say that the content of these products will change lives. There are all sorts of promises made about how different and how much better your life can be.

Some of these people will make these purchases and then just put them away in cupboards, on shelves and on their laptops, desktops and tablets. And never look at them.

To any outsider this looks like a fantastic and inspiring collection of material and would probably make them think that that person was a genius. Who else would surround themselves with such great personal development resources? This person has to be very wise, surely!

I have heard several people describe the continuous purchasing of the huge range of self-help and development books as "Shelf-Help."

The mistaken idea that just the purchase of the right product will create significant change and advancement.

Then there are those that buy this material and do look at it. These people hope that the activity of just reading the book or listening to or watching the course will change them. If reading a particular book hasn't changed that person or their situation then they go and find the next book that they think might be the one that actually changes them.

They end up with a very impressive bookshelf but very little positive change in the way they operate and how they respond to the challenges and opportunities in their life.

I went through a phase like this when I had no idea what I wanted to do with my life or my work. It was costly and only gave me some temporary relief from my challenges.

There is a massive difference between therapy and progress.

When you absorb any of the self-help materials it can make you feel better. You can recognise yourself described in the pages of the book. You can see that there is a way out. You can see that it leads to a really good place, a place where you would want to be. But if all I do is absorb the material all I am giving myself is temporary therapy.

So shelf-help is a relatively futile activity. The only benefits being, books on a book shelf look nice and you might impress visitors with your book collection.

When I got a little more focussed I realised that if I was going to benefit from these books and courses I needed to put these ideas into action to make some progress. I needed to **practice**.

I remember when I was a market research manager and looking to get better and better at the way I delivered the results of projects.

I would read lots of different books and find ideas that fitted into how I viewed the world. The big mistake I made early on, and on a few occasions, was to try and apply these ideas into an important presentation not long after having read them.

Usually they were ideas that I thought would be 'show stoppers'.

I would place so much emphasis on these new ideas that I would not know or practice the main findings, relying instead on a new idea to win everyone over.

How do you think that turned out?

Having not even practiced these new ideas out loud they would not be delivered how I thought they would. My audience would look confused or disinterested and my confidence would drop like a stone because the thing I thought would be the show stopper was a damp squib!

Furthermore, because I did not know the ins and outs of my project I floundered and each of these presentations felt like they would never end.

The good news was no one died and it only took a small number of these events to happen to me for me to realise that maybe I needed a new approach.

When I started my own business, I went on several different courses for NLP, hypnosis, voice skills and sales techniques amongst others.

The courses I went on we're experiential courses where the course leader introduced ideas followed by exercises where we could practice these techniques. A recurring theme was that although I had been told what to do and understood it, when I practiced I didn't get it right first time!

In fact it would take quite a few times to even get some elements of it right. There were barriers here and the series of courses helped me to understand that most of the barriers came from reinforced habits and behaviours which were my own.

Firstly, there was a hesitation to try anything if it wasn't going to be right first time.

My years of working in corporate companies, in what felt like competitive cultures, working with people who found it easier to tell me what was wrong with my thought or idea than to find what was right, meant I was hesitant to try unless I thought I could really do it.

Failure was not an option! So this meant I would have a long list of things I would want to try but I would actually never start trying them!

The second barrier was giving up too quickly. I would try something new a couple of times and then say " no I can't do it, I'm sure there is something else on my list that's easier for me than this!"

I heard Paul Scheele say that to try to do something new and get it right, you have to do it for a minimum of 50 times.

Most adults will not even try something new 10 times, most will give up before 6.

If we put an adult mind into that of a baby about to walk, most babies would stop after the 6th time of falling over and say "no thanks, walking's not for me....I'm a crawler!"

Practice is the key to success. Practice is about findings lots of ways not to do something, before finding the ways that it works. It's about practicing until a new skill becomes an automatic way you respond, behave or speak.

The Four Stages of Learning outlined by Noel Burch in the 1970s are as follows:

Unconsciously incompetent - in short, we don't know what we don't know.

Consciously incompetent - we now know there is something that we can't do very well.

Consciously Competent - there is something we do well but we need to pay a lot of attention to do it well. And finally....

Unconsciously Competent - we're good at something without even thinking about it.

If you think about it, anything that you're really good at now had to go through those four stages.

So where are we?

We're keen to learn and apply new skills, we know that if we are going to get very good at these we need to practice and we need to make mistakes. And we know that we are interested in making progress and spotting things that are us at our best.

The secret is how do we make all these mistakes and still retain credibility with the people who are important to us. How do we avoid seriously embarrassing failures that we allow to haunt us?

The answer is very simple we find and use opportunities for no-risk and low risk practice. That is practice that you can do where you take away the pressure of failure.

If you fail while doing this type of practice it is a sign of progress. A sign that you have tried something different.

This is a very good thing indeed!

I'll give you four top examples of how you can practice in situations that are no risk or low risk to you, there are thousands more:

Training courses

If you're on a training course you have the luxury of being in a room with people in the same position as you. They are there to learn new ideas and techniques and to practice them. Anytime you get an opportunity like this go for it!

Good trainers create an atmosphere that encourages people to try and allows them to fail in pursuit of understanding ideas and being able to work with them.

Nothing is more reassuring for a fellow class mate than realising they are not the only one feeling apprehensive about making mistakes.

These courses are designed to help you to get better at the way you deliver. Knowing a subject so that you can answer questions about it seems like a waste of time. If a course equips you to answer a multiple choice quiz on the subject then how much better off are you?

Always get full value for your courses by throwing yourself in. It will be scary at first but the more you do it the easier it gets.

The main reason so much training is ineffective is that people do not practice what they learn and so that knowledge is rarely if ever applied in a situation where the training attendee might benefit.

Lots of really good courses will provide you with or allow you to buy follow up material that will remind you of the content and help you to continue your practice beyond the dates of the course. Do you remember Ebbinghaus from Chapter 4?

Informal peer groups

If you attend a training course often there are people that you get on with and may even live reasonably close to you.

I have found that having gone through the challenge of practicing and failing with strangers, this lowers the barriers to practice and these people create a positive environment and are a good source for additional no-risk practice.

You will probably also find that these people are very keen to keep up their own practice, so it's win-win.

You may also find in your work or social circles, people who have done the same or similar courses but have faltered for lack of practice and lack of people to practice with.

Conversations with likeminded people can often throw up shared areas of interest and will create opportunities for you to practice.

Informal practice groups offer a cheap and risk free way to practice and hone your skills. The extra benefits are that these groups may also bring fresh ideas from other courses, books and videos that they have seen.

In my own experience good courses have contained great and inspirational trainers, good material and ideas and attendees who introduce you to new people and new sources for development.

Learning should be fun, set up the right environment with like-minded people and it will be.

Pecha-Kucha

There are lots of groups all around the world that give people like you a chance to practice their public speaking with supportive people around them.

For me, one of the most interesting of recent years is Pecha-Kucha. It's pronounced as Per-Catch-Ka and translates from Japanese to 'chit-chat'.

In the early 2000s Astrid Klein and Mark Dytham ran a business in japan called Klein Dytham Architecture. The architecture industry is like many others in that it has a very broad quality range when it comes to presenting. Klein and Dytham offered a creative space in their offices for other architects to come and present.

They were aware that if you give some architects that opportunity they will bore an audience for as long as they can. Never underestimate some people's inability to notice that they are delivering a snorefest. So Klein and Dytham introduced some rules. The key rule was the 20 x 20 rule.

All presentations will have 20 slides and each slide will be visible for 20 seconds. The slide will be automated so that you press go at the start and the slides will move when they move. Each presentation lasting 6 minutes and 40 seconds.

The great thing about this format is that it challenges you to tell your story in a relatively short time. It gets you into the habit of understanding what are the important things that you really need to communicate to move your audience.

Once this format took off it started to go viral. Chapters have been set up in cities all around the world. Klein Dytham supports the events and their aim is to have only one chapter per city. The chances are there is a Pecha-Kucha Night somewhere near to you.

At these events topics tend to be around things the presenters love or are inspired by. They might be showing some of their own work. They may be talking about hobbies or collections, they might share some great photography. There are a whole range of subjects covered.

Sometimes it's a range of topics in a single evening then at other times there is a central theme.

The events I've been to are organised by PKN Coventry. They are very enjoyable events, most are evening events with the occasional lunchtime event thrown in.

It's great to see people with a wide range of experience and confidence get up and take the opportunity to practice. I see so many different styles. Each one I've been to I've left with a little bit more knowledge but also a very positive feeling about just how good an organisation this is.

If you are someone who really wants to get better and better at your presentation performance, then this is too good an opportunity for you to miss. Start by finding your local group by visiting pechakucha.org and then go along to your first night as an audience member. I guarantee you it won't t take you too long before you feel inspired to have a go yourself.

The atmosphere is relaxed and these events seem to attract good-hearted, supportive people who are ideal for you to practice with. And at the same time you are reinforcing the principle of developing concise and audience focussed presentations.

Using Dictaphone and video

When there is no one else around to practice with, practicing on your own and out loud can be very helpful. The key thing here is to record your efforts and listen or watch back.

Many clients I have worked with have an aversion to seeing themselves or hearing their own voices. The echo of our voice through our own head means that what we hear is different from what everyone else hears.

Get use to watching and hearing yourself but there is one very useful tip when doing this.

When you watch or listen back play the role of your own coach. Play the role of someone who would like to help you. You will help yourself a lot more by doing this.

Sometimes the way we talk to ourselves in our own head is not how we would talk to someone else, especially if we want to help them.

So when you listen back, listen out for the elements of your practice that works. If you are doing something right, practicing that so that it works unconsciously will benefit you more than listing the 101 things that you didn't like.

In terms of equipment most phones, tablets and laptops have the capability to audio or video record you. It's worth doing and success, no matter how small is a great encourager for trying more.

Using social occasions

The fourth idea is to make the most of some social situations. I say some because we all need a break occasionally.

All of the great listening skills I have learned that have significantly increased the quality of my previously 'typically masculine' listening skills have been honed from low key social situations.

I practiced active listening without informing my friends what I was doing. As my books and training material had said, I would be very conscious of the techniques but my friends would be oblivious to them.

The more I practiced and cut the chatter in my own head and actually listened, the better I got at it and the more helpful I was to clients, friends and family.

When practicing the listening technique from Chapter 7. The way I would practice socially is to first find a couple of opportunities for repeating their words back as questions. Then the rest of the conversation would be normal conversation.

The more I practiced the more times I would try to use it in a single conversation. And the more I use it the better I get and the more effective it is.

I have lost count of the number of times that people have complemented me on my conversational skills, when I have been mainly using the repeating words technique throughout the conversation.

In truth, most people's idea of a great conversation is one in which they talk and the other person listens. At the very least your social practice is providing a public service!

One of the other things that I found particularly useful was to learn mind reading card tricks. This was good for a number of reasons. Firstly carrying a pack of playing cards round with me was quite easy to do.

Secondly there are plenty of social situations where one or two people are interested in a bit of mind reading.

Thirdly a trick done well can add some value to your friends and colleagues. It gives them something to talk about or have a laugh about.

And you have had a chance to practice listening and focussing and it has actually added to the evening rather than making you feel like you have asked for a favour from your friends and colleagues.

There are plenty of relatively simple mind reading tricks that are fun to do and give you the opportunity to listen, and then read someone in terms of voice, tone and body language.

This all adds to your instinctive listening skills.

Another skill that I practice in social situations is memory feats. Using the memory technique in Chapter 4 I have created a 52 place journey that allows me to learn the order of a shuffled pack of playing cards.

Once I create the journey I then use things and people to represent cards. For example; the 3 of clubs.

C is the third letter of the alphabet and C is the first letter of clubs. So I look for someone whose initials are CC and my first thought is Charlie Chaplin.

Dustin Hoffman is my 4 of hearts, Ed Sheeran is my 5 of Spades. For Aces it's Alan Carr for my Ace of Clubs, Ann

Diamond for my Ace of Diamonds and then I use associations for my other two aces Asa Hartford (an ex-Manchester City & West Bromwich Albion footballer) is my Ace of Hearts and it can only be Motorhead for the Ace of Spades. For me anyway!

I hope that is enough examples and the more you use the memory technique the easier this will be to do.

The first time I did this it took me about half an hour to create a 52 place journey, it then took me about the same time to create all my people and connections.

The more I do this the better I get. I can now learn the order of a deck of cards in about 10 or 15 minutes. There are people who can do this in a couple of minutes but that says to me that they are maybe not making the best use of their lives or maybe they compete in a lot of memory competitions.

If someone correctly recalled the order of a randomly ordered deck of cards then that in itself is quite a feat. And I would suspect that you would be very impressed.

I was a little unsure if I could do this at first. The first time I did it I realised the impact it had on other people. When I returned to them and rightly predicted each card before it was turned over I received a lot of sounds of amazed people.

It firstly demonstrates to you the power of your own memory. Secondly you can honestly tell other people that if they want a good memory they can have one. And thirdly you will have again provided a nice bit of entertainment.

Another great use of this technique is teaching it to others. Once you have practiced this a number of times and you have really pushed yourself (like the deck of cards) you will feel that you can use it to help others.

I have used it to help people pass exams. And a whole range of different exam subjects; Physics, mathematics, history, law and many others.

Not only have I helped people to pass their exams but they now have a technique they can use for life.

The other thing I have done is to teach this to people to increase their confidence. There are a number of people who think their memory is fading and that this is a very clear sign of their inevitable demise.

In our modern lives new gadgets are being developed and sold all with the aim of making our lives easier. The mobile phone is one of the best examples.

If I want someone's phone number they can just send it as a text, my phone will accept it and add it to my address book and at no time have I actually heard or learned their number.

They can text all sorts of information that I can store and only ever access it for the few times I need it.

Modern gadgetry is removing opportunities for us to use our memory.

When I was a boy I had to remember all my friends' phone numbers in my head. I then went round the corner to the phone box and rang them.

There was lots of information that I needed to remember because I didn't have a gadget for it.

I am a big gadget fan and I love what these devices do.

However, I also believe that memory is like muscle and that it doesn't work as well for you if you do not use it.

So I find as many purposes as I can for using my memory to keep my mind active.

For those of you who have a good memory you will remember that before I was talking about gadgets I was talking about using memory to increase people's confidence.

Teaching this technique to people has demonstrated to them that they still have good memorys. All they need is a purpose and a good technique and this will make it work really well for them. That is something that I have seen make people recover their confidence in themselves. Now someone as human spirited as yourself has to think that would be a great thing to do.

Storytelling also offers many social situations for no risk, low risk practice.

With your drink of choice in hand and a group of friends around you, telling stories is a wonderful pastime. You can practice funnelling to get their focus and attention. You can try out your version of stories that you have read about. And you can practice adding rich detail to stories to make them more engaging.

Storytelling is common no matter what age you are and from where in the world you come from. You will all know people who you hold up as good storytellers and you will know the pleasure you have had from their stories.

The more you practice this the more you can bring this format and thinking into your work presentations.

So what happens if you do make a mistake?

In the social scenario if someone thinks your behaviour is odd and asks you "what's up?" then it's quite easy in that company to tell them what you are doing. I've found my friends to be very supportive and often interested to try things for themselves.

Practice is the key! The more you practice the closer you get to being unconsciously competent.

Give yourself the best chance of improving your outcomes by being really well practiced before you put a new technique into something that really matters to you.

And remember, to quote Peter Thomson, "practice doesn't make perfect, perfect practice makes perfect!"

You need a lot of practice to make these ideas work for you.

Make it no-risk or low risk!

Actions:

Take the opportunity to practice new presentation ideas at or with the following:

Training courses

Informal peer groups

Dictaphone and video

Pecha-Kucha or public speaking groups

Social occasions

Chapter 14
Getting Feedback & Excelling At Q&A

The great thing about presenting yourself at meetings and presentations is that there is usually no end of people who are happy to give you their feedback.

Feedback is essential to anyone who wants to do better and anyone who wants to get effective results. The challenge with all that feedback is that a lot of it is often unhelpful.

As an effective presenter you are interested in a number of key areas of feedback. One is from your primary and secondary audience and the second key one is anyone who you have primed before your presentation.

There is a third area of useful feedback and that is the employment of technology. If you are able to audio or video record your presentation and review it back later, this can be very, very useful. More about that later.

So first let's tackle our primary and secondary audience.

After a presentation try to find an opportunity to talk to the people you have just communicated with. Now that you are practicing the strategy for an effective presentation you will have put together some very clear outcomes.

You will know what you want them to think feel or do as a result of your communication. So the questions you ask are easy. You first need to understand who they are and then ask them what do they think, feel or what will they do as a result of your communication.

I write this as a very simple thing because this is a very simple thing. If you have prepared well then you will know what you want your feedback to be.

I have lost count the number of times where somebody's post communication question is "how did I do?"

The answers to this question are numerous.
"You were brilliant!"
"I wouldn't have done it that way!"
"I enjoyed it."
"It was a bit long."
"You didn't tell them about our other ideas"
"You didn't look scared"
"You did it better than I could"
"You did really well, how did I do?"

All of the above is feedback but to you and I it's mostly useless. It might temporarily boost or deflate our egos but it does nothing to help us get any closer to knowing have we wasted people's time or have we actually done something worthwhile for them.

The last comment (you did really well, how did I do?") reminds me of my time presenting at conferences for Adams Childrenswear.

I would be one of about a dozen presenters at the big events that were held once or twice a year. At the end of the presentations we would get together like some sort of self-esteem support group.

I'd say to one of my colleagues "your presentation was really good" and he'd say "and so was yours." It was the polite thing to do, it was a nice thing to do but it was ultimately unhelpful.

After all I had subjected an audience to half an hour of standard PowerPoint slides with little adaptation from the original pack designed for an interactive meeting. I'd talked at them and thrown out a selection of ideas that left them ultimately making their mind up about what if any of it was relevant or important to them. I probably also sent out a variety of conflicting messages without a clear single direction.

If after the event they were not doing what I thought I'd told them they needed to do to improve the customer experience, then it was all too easy for me to blame them for not listening.

My wake-up call came after one retail conference where I spent my coffee breaks and lunchtime with a number of store managers I knew.

They were very complimentary about my presentation. But what was most telling was that as a result of my presentation they were going to talk to every customer who came in the store as soon as they came through the door. They were really clear that that was what they had to do.

I'd have been very happy with that response except it was exactly what I was warning them away from. What I had wanted them to do was for members of staff to be aware of customers coming in and then to make a point of making eye contact with them and smiling at them.

Any conversation was to be initiated by the customer and if the customer wanted to talk, the smile and eye contact was enough to make them feel comfortable enough to approach the member of staff

At previous events we, as speakers, were very good at passing the blame for lack of understanding on the attention span or capability of the audience. However, I knew these managers as very intelligent people and people that were enthusiastic about their roles. When I looked back at my presentation, I could see how they could have misunderstood, actually how I had miscommunicated.

In my efforts to tell them about how much information I had, I neglected to notice that that level of information was unnecessary at this forum and the sheer volume of information and individual ideas created a high likelihood of ambiguity.

20 minutes with my target audience and their feedback was a bigger catalyst for me to improve my communication skills than hours of talking with my peers at our 'we're all nice guys and a good support group' sessions.

Getting feedback from your target audience makes all the difference. Make a point of actively seeking it. The great thing about it is if you have done that you will know whether your presentation went well or not.

If someone else that is not your target audience tells you it could have been better, you can make them aware that your job was to communicate a particular message to your audience and from asking them it is clear that they have understood that message.

You can tell thank them for their feedback but as an effective presenter you are interested in getting your results to line up correctly with your objectives.

How to Make Your Q&A Add to Your Communication

Some sessions allow for chances to have questions asked during or after the session. One of the things you need to think about is if you are having questions how does that best work for you, during or after.

Sometimes you will ask for questions at the end of the session. Sometimes you will be happy to have questions during the session.

Again your objectives will guide you as to what is the right choice for a particular presentation.

Questions at the end are nice and simple because it does not interrupt the flow of a planned presentation. If you want to take questions during a presentation, it is sensible to only ask questions directly connected with what you are talking about now.

If I am taking questions during a presentation I will usually specify that I will answer any questions that are related about understanding the topic I am talking about.

Any unrelated questions will be taken at the end.

I will also make a point of asking people to hold onto their questions if it relates to something that I know is included in my presentation later on.

Some important points when dealing with Q&A:

Listen: Let your audience ask their question and do not start answering their question until they have finished. By listening properly you are in a position to both answer the question well and also influence your audience more about you and your content.

Compliment: If someone asks a good question let them know it was a good question. It makes the questioner feel better, it makes you look better and it can often guide an audience about what is the right level of question for them to pitch.

Read the Questioner: If someone asks a difficult question and displays high level of enthusiasm for their question, then you might want to say something like "it appears to me you might already have some views, can you tell me them?"

This allows you extra time to listen to the views and for your answer to be a comment on their thoughts. It both allows you to answer a difficult question and increases your likeability by giving someone else a chance to shine.

Always answer in the first sentence: When you are asked a question, there are few things more irritating to an audience than someone waffling and appearing to avoid answering the question.

Answer the question in your first sentence then elaborate as much as is necessary.

If someone asks "Are you the right person?" the answer is "Yes." Then elaborate.

Controversial Questions: Some questions require talking about relatively classified information or are too complicated for a yes/no type response in particular audiences.

Deal with these head on. Tell the audience this is not right for this forum. And suggest an alternative time or venue when this could be answered.

And if you don't know, you don't know: If you are asked a question you don't know or haven't thought about, often the best answer is "I don't know but I can find out for you."

Fudging an answer can often lead to unravelling good work you have done in your presentation. Be calm, be strong and be honest. It will pay off for you.

It's always helpful to adopt an attitude of thinking your audience is asking questions out of interest rather than thinking they are trying to catch you out.

Consider you and the audience as one group that want to move forward and the question process is a way of moving that group forward together.

If you start with a good attitude you will tend to be a little more relaxed. When you are more relaxed you tend to be more open, you can listen better and you will be comfortable enough to take time to consider questions before answering them.

Consideration before answering tends to bring better more concise answers. It also demonstrates to an audience that you have listened to their question and you are giving it serious consideration. This can increase the perception of the quality of the answer that you give.

If you have an important presentation coming up ask a friend or colleague to randomly ask you the sorts of questions that you think you may be asked. Audio record the session and write down really good answers it is amazing how many times your practice questions will actually come up in Q&A sessions.

The more you practice the easier it is to respond.

Actions:

Actively pursue feedback from your target audiences after your presentations

Be wary of feedback from your colleagues if it does not reflect the response of your target audience

Practice Q&A technique and listening skills

Chapter 15
A Few Thoughts On Writing

I am not a natural writer and the writing of this book has been a challenging experience. It has taken me way longer to write this book than I originally thought.

Knowing what to put in and knowing what to leave out has been an interesting challenge. Finding the time on top of a busy work schedule has proved difficult. There have been times when I have thoroughly enjoyed writing the book. And there have been times when it has been like wading through waist high porridge!

At a point where I was prepared just to give up on the idea, I found some inspirational information and also was given some great advice. For those of you that are interested in writing a book but are experiencing some of my challenges I offer you a couple of bits of advice.

The first one is to find out how lots of other people go about writing books and scripts. A great place to start is a couple of programmes called 'Screenwipe' by the Guardian columnist and author Charlie Brooker.

In these programmes he talks to a range of authors and screenwriters. People like Russell T Davies, Paul Abbott, Jesse Armstrong & Sam Bain, Graham Linehan and Tony Jordan. They all write about a variety of different subjects and, most interestingly, they all have their own approaches to how they think of content and how they go about their writing process.

I picked up a lot of handy hints and the great thing about these programmes was that there were a lot of ideas that were interesting but definitely not me and lots of things which made me think I should try that.

I found these programmes on YouTube and they were still on there the last time I looked. So I highly recommend this.

The second tip is the one which has been the most helpful to me. It was an idea given to me by Peter Thomson. He told me about a simple technique that you sit down in a nice comfy chair with a drink of your choice and a Dictaphone and you dictate your book.

When I first started working for myself in 1997 I bought some dictation software to save me money on typing fees. In 1997 this technology was not at its best. Most times I used it I would be left with a page of totally incomprehensible rubbish.

Last year I bought the latest version of Dragon Dictation software. The improvement has been considerable. I can talk into my Dictaphone, connect it directly to my computer and let it play.

Then Dragon will happily turn my words into text. It still requires me to sit down afterwards and check and edit but it does take most of the work out of the typing.

As someone who is much more comfortable talking than writing it works really well for me.

I use Dragon; I haven't investigated any other software or apps because Dragon does what I need it to do. I'm sure there are plenty of other good software and apps that will do the job and more.

Another option is to dictate and then give it to a typing service to get typed up. Choose whichever works for you.

I have also encountered a number of freelance copywriters who have offered to ghost write the book. That was an interesting idea but in the end I chose to use the dictation system.

These are just a couple of ideas but it does demonstrate if you think you have a book in you, then there are a whole lot of methods to turn that book into something physical.

Good luck

Chapter 16
Next Steps

If you only picked this book up in the hope of a getting a guide or answer to an immediate communication problem I hope that the book has been of help to you and maybe we'll meet again when your next problem arises.

If you have read all the way through because you are interested in continually pushing the best performance of you then again I hope this has been of help to you and it's now time to think; what next?

This book covers a lot of areas for you to consider how to deliver better and more effective communication. I don't offer finite answers because I believe it's all about your ability to ask good questions, assess the responses and then to have a range of possible responses.

The more adaptable you are the more success you will have.

Earlier in the book I said that I have learned a huge amount in the time I have been studying communication but at the same time I felt there was lots more that I am yet to learn.

I find that thought exciting and compelling. I hope you, as an enthusiastic communicator, feel the same. In the next section I have listed some references; speakers, authors and books, all of which go into greater detail on a number of the subjects I have talked about.

I advise you to always be driven on interest. Any of the areas that you have interest in will probably bring you the best results.

Interest usually means that your work will rarely feel like work and will make your research and practice so much more enjoyable.

There are so many fantastic and inspirational people and topics out there and I hope you have the same joy that I have in finding out and trying out these ideas.

As with anyone else I work with I do hope that this book has made a difference for you in some way. And thank you for your time, it's been a pleasure working with you.

Further Reading

Below are a few people whose writing and training material has been very beneficial along the way for me. There are lots more out there but if you are unsure take a look out at these.

Peter Thomson: "the Achievers edge." This is a monthly audio newsletter. It has great interviews, fantastic hints and tips about many facets of business life and the monthly format gives you time to do something with last month's great ideas before you get more added next month.

This has been my audio mentor since I started out on my own. It has introduced me to really great people, books and programmes and I would count it as one of the key foundations for my success.

I started listening to this in 1997. The programmes from then I can still listen to and they still provide great ideas. The price is great too!

I have had the good fortune to meet Peter on several occasions and he is constantly introducing me to new ideas and always offers a new perspective to look at older ideas.

Dominic O'Brien: "Quantum Memory Power." This is the Nightingale Conant programme that taught me a lot about memory. I have read some other great authors but this is where I started and I still think the programme is a really good one.

He has also written a number of books if you want to dip your toe into some other memory techniques. For memory I would also recommend **Christiane Stenger's** "A Sheep falls Out Of The Tree." And "Moonwalking With Einstein" by **Joshua Foer.**

Joshua Foer is a speaker that features on **TED.com** this is a site that features some great talks from the fields of science, technology, the arts and business.

I guarantee you when you look through the index on this site you will find speakers and subjects that could be of real interest to you.

If you are unsure where to start I would recommend:

Dan Ariely
Ken Robinson
Shukla Bose
Patti Maes
Malcolm Gladwell

There is also a great talk from **Tony Robbins**. And I would recommend his material if you are looking for a bit of inspiration. His story about Sylvester Stallone and Rocky is a great example of how to take a less well known story and turn it into a meaningful story for so many.

What I like most about that story is I know people who think that Sylvester Stallone has little or no talent. That story has made them dramatically reconsider. It's a great story and he has many others.

If anyone has an interest in hypnosis I can heartily recommend **Igor Ledochowski**. I had done a number of NLP courses before realising that I was more interested in hypnosis than NLP. I went on a number of courses for hypnosis and read some books. It was Igor's training that helped me to really get to grips with hypnosis.

He understood how to train people on the subtleties and nuances of hypnosis that make a difference. His courses on conversational hypnosis are also excellent.

If your preference is NLP there are two reference books that I tend to use more than others. One is "NLP Workbook" by **Joseph O Conner** and the other is "NLP At Work" by **Sue Knight**.

Michael J Gelb has written a number of good books that I really like; "Present Yourself" is a good guide on public speaking and he has written a lot of books on understanding genius. "How To Think Like Leonardo Da Vinci" is a very good read.

Richard Wiseman is a very good writer and tends to like to present ideas in a clear and concise way and is a keen myth buster. He has a lot of good books; I would first recommend "59 seconds" and then suggest you look at the rest of his catalogue.

Geoff Thompson is someone I have done some work with. Geoff's own life story is something that is worth hearing. He will tell you stories of going from a cleaner and a nightclub bouncer to teaching at Chuck Norris's school and becoming a BAFTA award winning screenwriter.

I would recommend "the Elephant and the Twig" as an introduction to Geoff's work.

In chapter 6 I talked about approaches to communicating across cultures. "Kiss, Bow or Shake Hands" by **Terri Morrison** and **Wayne A Conaway** is a good place to start and is useful if time is short.

I would also recommend "Cultural Intelligence" by **Brooks Peterson** particularly to those that want to learn more about working with other cultures.

On body language there are a lot of really good books. As a starter I would always suggest "The Definitive Book of Body Language" by **Allan and Barbara Pease**. It is an enjoyable read and covers a huge range of body language elements. I imagine that's why they named it the Definitive Book!

I haven't covered influence and persuasion in extensive detail because it is a major topic in its own right. Again there is a lot to explore in this area.

I would recommend as a starting point "Influence: Science And Practice" by **Robert Cialdini**. This is a great read and covers some really excellent ideas.

In the chapter about storytelling I talked about the idea of funnelling. One area where this is done exceptionally well is in mediumship and fortune telling. There are courses that will teach you these skills. Instead I would recommend an e-book that I read recently called "The James Bond Cold Reading" by **Julian Moore**. It's a quirky title but I think it shows many good examples of introducing general statements that make connections with audiences.

As long as you have an appetite for self-development you will always find a wealth of new and interesting ideas out there.

About the author

Bob Caren is a coach, a trainer, a speaker and a facilitator and has been running his own business for 15 years. He works with clients in agriculture, pharmaceutical, retailing, engineering, advertising, eventing, banking, hair and beauty, entertainment, consulting, education and design and production.

Bob trains and coaches people in presentation skills, selling, negotiation, persuasion and influence and organisational behaviour. He is a trained hypnotist.

You can contact Bob at robert.caren@virgin.net